Praise for Reclaiming Hope

"Marcy is the bees knees, one of the absolute best people I've had the privilege to work with. This book is so well written. It succinctly addresses the common needs and challenges of being in the system. I encourage any of my folks working in the child welfare system, or any curious about fostering/ adoption, to give this a read."

—Brett Watts, MS, MFT

"If you are an adoptive or foster parent or even a parent of bio kids, you will want to check this book out. I have been blessed time and again by Marcy's honesty, authenticity and compassionate heart! This book takes you right into the deep of her journey and somehow provides hope in the midst of the challenges!"

—Dorina Lazo Gilmore, author of Cora Cooks
Pancit and blogger for Self Talk the Gospel

"As a foster/adoptive parent of five, this is the most amazing book I have read about the subject. It is REAL. It should be a requirement for anyone considering this life. Marcy has been in the trenches and it shows. It offers encouragement for those of us who are there now. HIGHLY RECOMMENDED from an experienced been there/doing that foster/adoptive parent."

—Cynthia Kelly, Foster / Adoptive Mother

"*Marcy Pusey shares her story of fostering and adopting with such candor and heart. She doesn't sugarcoat the reality or gloss over the warts or romanticize the notion of growing a family through this avenue. Instead Marcy writes her story of loving her foster and adopted kids with a warrior spirit, and in doing so, other parents in her shoes are both being heard and being given a voice- a voice of courage, possibility, and hope. Marcy makes sure they know they are not alone.*"

—Hillary Tubin, Literacy Educator

"*I've adopted four children and fostered many more. I consider myself a "veteran" and yet I still learned a lot from this beautifully written, heart wrenching, inspiring book. Whether you are curious about adopting from foster care or a mom in the trenches, this book is an invaluable resource. "Reclaiming Hope" made me feel understood and encouraged. The author gave voice to things I've felt but didn't have the courage to admit for fear of judgment. She gets it! This book whispered into my heart "Be gentle with yourself, Mom." I am better for having read it.*"

—Kelly Greenawalt, Foster / Adoptive Mother

"*The book I wish I had twenty years ago when I began this journey! It is written from the heart and speaks the truth of the ups and downs of the foster/adoptive process! It is an awesome read that is valuable to those already in the foster/adoptive process, thinking about beginning their journey as well as their friends and family. Her insight and experience into this process is amazing. The additional input from others throughout the book gives many perspectives as well. It is a resource all foster/adoptive agencies should have!*"

—Janet Carpenter, Foster / Adoptive Mother

RECLAIMING
HOPE

MARCY PUSEY

Dear Julie,
Congrats! I hope
this book proves to be
a source of relief, hope,
and validation in every possible
way. ♡ *Marcy*

OVERCOMING THE CHALLENGES
OF PARENTING FOSTER
AND ADOPTED CHILDREN

Library of Congress Control Number
2016956615

Cover design by Happy Services

Editing by Wayne Purdin, Lead Editor of Wordsmithies

www.wordsmithies.com

Author photograph by
Allison Vasquez

Some names and identifying details have been changed to protect the privacy of individuals.

ISBN-10:0-9969637-0-7
ISBN-13:978-0-9969637-0-1

For orders, please visit

www.marcypusey.com

DEDICATION

To my four children, each one a gift and a joy.

I love you.

For you created my inmost being; you knit
me together in my mother's womb.
I praise you because I am fearfully and
wonderfully made; your works are
wonderful; I know that full well.

— Psalm 139:13-14 (NIV)

ACKNOWLEDGMENTS

This book wouldn't have happened without the love and support of my husband, Jeremy, and our children. My family has been gracious and patient as telling this story, our story, consumed many of my free moments.

I must also thank my community at Self Publishing School for their tireless support, constant stream of encouragement and feedback, and the hand-holding I sometimes needed to write, edit, design, and publish this book. I have made friends among you. Thank you!!!

Thank you, also, to the many individuals who shared their stories with me. I can't tell you how often I wanted to reach through the page and wrap you up in a hug. You feel like kindred souls to me and though I haven't met many of you, I hold you dearly. You are precious. Your story is a testimony of the beauty that comes from ashes, even while the embers still burn. You are a large part of why I am brave to tell my story. Thank you for your bravery.

Thank you for welcoming my voice.

TABLE OF CONTENTS

ACKNOWLEDGMENTS   7

INTRODUCTION   11

CHAPTER 1 : **You Are Not Alone**   17

CHAPTER 2 : **The Challenge of Beginning**   26

CHAPTER 3 : **The Challenge of the System**   33

CHAPTER 4 : **The Challenge of High Turnaround   42
Rates of Social Workers**

CHAPTER 5 : **The Challenge of Making Our Voices Heard** 49

CHAPTER 6 : **The Challenge of Being an Advocate**   55

CHAPTER 7 : **The Challenge of Red Tape**   65

CHAPTER 8 : **The Challenge of Misinformation**   74

CHAPTER 9 : **Recap of the Broken System**   81

CHAPTER 10 : **The Challenge of the Unknowns**   85

CHAPTER 11 : **The Challenge of Lack of Social Skills** 89

CHAPTER 12 : **The Challenge of Unknown Medical Issues**   97

CHAPTER 13 : **The Challenge of Emotional**   102
Delays and Blocks

CHAPTER 14 : **The Challenge of Bad Behavior**   111

CHAPTER 15 : **The Challenge of Parenting**   118

CHAPTER 16 : **The Challenge of Trauma Versus Typical**   125

CHAPTER 17 : **The Challenge of Their Attachment**   131

CHAPTER 18 : **The Challenge of Our Attachment**   137

CHAPTER 19 : **The Challenge of Family,**   146
Friends, and Community

CHAPTER 20 : **The Challenge of the Transient Life**   152

CHAPTER 21 : **The Challenge of Identity**   160

CHAPTER 22 : **The Challenge of Birth Family**   168

CHAPTER 23 : **The Challenge of Our Birth Children**   174

CHAPTER 24 : **The Challenge of Secondary Trauma**   182

CHAPTER 25 : **Conclusion**   193

ABOUT THE AUTHOR   199

INTRODUCTION

"What's next is for the rest of us—jaded but experienced adoptive parents and the adoption professionals who surround us (often adoptive parents themselves) to stop relying on adoption education and social workers to convey the darker realities of attachment disorders, institutional delays, and post-adoption depression and start talking about them ourselves."

—Louisa Leontiades, Five Hard Truths About Adoption Adoptive Parents Don't Want to Hear

When eight-year-old Michael joined our family, I had a three-month-old baby. Michael had lived in a foster home with a single foster mother, his older sister, and two younger brothers, along with a couple of teenage girls. During a squabble with his two little brothers (ages six and seven at the time), he threatened to kill them. Being a foster child, his foster mom had to report his threat in case he ever acted on it.

That day, he went to school like any other day. However, at the end of school, the social worker was there to pick him up, all of his stuff in garbage bags in her trunk. She brought him to my house, a stranger's house.

The eighth stranger's house he'd move to in his three short years in foster care.

His hair was gelled into spikes like Sonic the Hedgehog. He had big eyes and was quiet. He had NO idea that his life was about to flip upside down once again. He didn't even get to say goodbye to his brothers and sister.

I offered him a snack and something to drink. That night, at bedtime, he went to sleep with the lamp shining on his face and the radio on. He did this for months.

Actually, Michael was only supposed to be with us for the weekend, while the System figured out whether it was safe enough for his brothers to live with him. During this time, the foster mom presented a list of ways he disrupted the home. He was impulsive, abusive to the younger children, was two grade levels behind in school, didn't listen, on and on. As a single woman trying to parent all of these foster kids, she couldn't do it with his additional struggles. She felt that his absence from the home would settle many of the challenges that arose.

I didn't understand this and I judged her. When Michael told me how much time he'd spent grounded at her house, I decided she lacked the resources and strategies to parent him well. We decided we could do better and asked to keep him.

I understand how arrogant this was, and I'm embarrassed to acknowledge it. Give it a few years, and Michael would find himself just as often grounded in our home, with my strategy-filled self at a complete dearth of ideas on how to parent this child. I found so much grace for his previous foster mother. I felt bad about my previous judgments. This kid was *hard work*.

Yeah, he had A LOT to work on. He didn't know how to sit in a chair. He couldn't follow directions to save his life (and seemed clueless about how, not rebellious). There was a time we picked him up from an event; all of the kids were sitting down, listening to the leader... except Michael. He was hopping around the edges of the room, as though he was the only exception to the rule. He saw us arrive and smiled big and waved. He didn't even know how to pretend to follow the rules to stay out of trouble.

He wouldn't stop eating. If he had the opportunity, he would eat everything in sight... even to the point of throwing up. He had panic attacks if he saw needles (i.e., during vaccinations). He talked incessantly. And, probably the thing that got to me the most... he followed me EVERYWHERE.

I'm an introvert and very content with quiet, private places. But Michael seemed to think he was doing me a favor by always keeping me company. I realized it was because he never wanted to be alone. Sending him to his room was the worst possible consequence. Extra chores? Not bad if he could be around people. But he was also funny and very charming.

He was little and needed help... and we could help him.

Or so we thought.

Too many people become foster and adoptive parents without having accurate information or knowing what to expect. Of those who do, many find they don't have the resources or support they need to do it well. Many parents find themselves inadequate and incapable of performing the task of parenting foster and adopted kids. These parents are often unable to find the help they need or are too embarrassed to look.

The reality of parenting these kids is much harder than the promo videos, trainings, and fliers claim. Pre-adoption information is scant and misleading while post adoption support is almost nonexistent. Parenting biological children is hard enough! But taking in children burdened with trauma and loss can be devastating for everyone.

But it doesn't have to be that way. Adoption can be a beautiful, wonderful experience for you and your family. It will be hard. But it doesn't have to be devastating.

This book is designed to tell you the truth about adopting, fostering, and taking guardianship of children in a new and easy to understand way. I've gathered the ten greatest challenges, as revealed through my own experience as a foster mother, adoptive mother, and counselor as well as from what people have shared in surveys, messages, and conversations. This book helps to clear up misinformation fed to prospective foster and adoptive parents in a concise and easy-to-read manner. This is the stuff they don't tell you during the interview or orientation. This book is for the family or parent who question their decision to foster or adopt. For the person dealing with regret, loss, and disappointment. For those hoping to be better prepared for the struggles they'll face.

You are not alone.

Chapter 19 is helpful for the friend or family member who wants to support adoptive/foster families.

If you are considering foster parenting or adopting, are already in it and drowning, or want to throw a lifesaver to a foster parenting/adoptive friend, then this is your must-read.

I have spent the last sixteen years working between Child Protective Services, group homes for teenage males and teenage mothers, wrap-around programs, community based services, foster agencies, and as a behavior analyst for children with autism, emotional disturbances, and developmental delays.

My husband has worked in low performing schools where many of the children are in single-parent families or foster homes. We came to our decision to foster and adopt with an incredible amount of experience and knowledge, and still we've been surprised, challenged, and yes, at times, regretful. We've read tons of books and articles, watched video after video, and had countless conversation on the subject of adoption and foster parenting.

Did you know that about twenty percent of all adoptions are "disrupted" before they're finalized? That means that one out of every five children who start the adoption process with a family ends up remaining in foster care, the orphanage, or the group home. America's underground market for adopted children, a loose Internet network of desperate parents seeking new homes for kids they regret adopting, is disturbingly on the rise.[1]

We have no idea how many adopted kids end up being passed from home to home after adoption. That doesn't even include the families who keep the children but who struggle deeply with attachment issues, continued Child Protective Services involvement, academic failures, social ostracizing, post-adoption depression, and divorce or marital struggles.

We are convinced that breaking down information barriers in the early process, aligning expectations with reality, and being surrounded with healthy support will lead to a successful foster family/adoption experience. Many people have already experienced the great encouragement found in this helpful book on preparing for their child, thriving while raising them, and giving them back to society as productive and healthy contributing members, while keeping their own sanity all the while.

But don't take my word for it, take Janet's. "After thirteen foster children, three foster-adoptions, and three fosterguardianships, my only regret is lack of support from the county. The child who gave me the run for my money I got at fourteen months; nevertheless, she is now in the Army Reserve and a wonderful mother to two beautiful boys."

With this book, you will be better equipped to make the daily foster-adopt decisions, have the courage to stand by those decisions when it gets hard, and know how to lighten the load for friends and family who've adopted, thus contributing to a better world for all of us.

Don't end up disillusioned, heart-broken, and full of regret for doing a good thing. Don't miss out on an opportunity to love caring for your blended family. Don't be blinded by misinformation, humiliation, or lack of support. Be the kind of foster or adoptive family other people see and say, "Wow, adoption is really beautiful. How can I be part of it?" Be the kind of person who takes action to have a healthy, whole family now.

Each chapter will give you new insight and encouragement into what it takes to be a healthy foster/adoptive family. Take control of your situation right now; make informed decisions, and enjoy the new life and family you're creating.

---

1. Megan Twohey, "Americans Use the Internet to Abandon Children Adopted from Overseas," Reuters Investigates, September 9, 2013, accessed October 8, 2015, www. reuters.com/investigates/adoption/#article/part1

CHAPTER 1

You Are Not Alone

"Those who overcome great challenges will be changed, and often in unexpected ways. For our struggles enter our lives as unwelcome guests, but they bring valuable gifts. And once the pain subsides, the gifts remain. These gifts are life's true treasures, bought at great price, but cannot be acquired in any other way."

—Steve Goodier, author

We definitely don't need another place to hear how hard parenting adoptive and foster kids is. We live it every day. That's not what this book is about.

This book is about naming those challenges, sharing in each other's stories, each other's comforts and struggles, and encouraging one another along, so that we can love and enjoy the families we've chosen. I believe that when we name something, we have actively acknowledged it. And suddenly, the monster that's been terrorizing our hearts and minds seems more manageable. Rumplestiltskin, a character of the Brothers Grimm, figured this out, didn't he? If he could get your name, he could control you.

While I don't believe you'll be able to control all of these challenges just by having a name for them, I *do* believe that with more information you'll be equipped with the tools to confront the challenges you're up against. Or, better yet, how to use what you're up against for some good.

These are challenges. Some are harder to overcome than others. But none of them are insurmountable.

They are also opportunities.

And I'm going to share with you the lessons we've learned along the way, the problems that have nearly flattened us, and the way we've seen (and continue to hope for) good in each one.

I speak from our own experience, in which we still live every day. I don't claim to have all of the answers.

This is the story of our hearts and our adventure, and we know how good it feels when someone says, "Hey, I get it. You are not alone."

The following is who we are as a family and as individuals and why you can take our word for it, why you can count us among your people, among the voices in your life speaking truth and encouragement and comfort.

Even though we'd spent many years working with foster and adoptive families, it wasn't until we stepped into it ourselves that we could really understand the nuances of taking in a stranger's child and loving them. And when I say, "loving" them, I don't simply mean feeling love for them. That comes and goes with the wind, as any of us who've ever been in a relationship knows. I mean the act of choosing to love them. Of course, when we feel the love, the choice is easier to make.

When my husband leaves me a sweet note and flowers, love flutters up in my heart and I want to express it in return. When the romance gets lost in the diapers and meetings and careers and endless to-dos… love becomes our choice. This is no different than inviting a child into your home and making them your own. For some, the feeling of love is instantaneous. They feel a connection, a deep soul-attachment to this child. They feel a supernatural involvement bringing them together. Regardless of who birthed this child, he or she was always meant to be theirs.

This was not my story.

I love kids, don't get me wrong. But I worked with them for about an hour and then I went home. Or I held someone's baby, then handed them back. I was not the little girl hoping and dreaming and preparing for that "One day when I'm a mommy." I wanted to get married and have kids, but it wasn't my purpose for living. So when we decided to begin fostering, it wasn't at all about meeting a personal need to have children. It was purely about our WHY, which I share in detail in the final chapter.

We saw the need and wanted to be a part of the solution. We wanted to live authentic lives within our faith practices and beliefs, caring for the "orphans and widows in distress." We wanted to share the love and comfort God has given us with others. These were the reasons we decided to actively practice love to children and families who were lost in a system.

We knew that certifying for foster care and adoption takes FOREVER, so we started early. We chose to work with a great agency that offered support, trainings, and more one-on-one time than the county could offer us.

As life sometimes has it, by the time our certification was done, I was pregnant with our first child. We were legally certified to take in foster children and I was months away from giving birth.

Our first child was born in August.

Our first call came in November.

We were given a choice between two children: one who had a serious past with sexual-abuse and one who didn't. We chose the latter. We were clear in our certification process that, because we would have other young children in the home, we didn't want to take in any children who'd exhibited or experienced sexual trauma. Of course, I now realize that would have filtered out the majority of foster children.

That's when Michael joined us.

One month later, we took in Gina, a thirteen-year-old with a three-month-old baby. My baby was four-months-old by this time. We thought that I could model for her how to be a good new mom. Looking back... how crazy was that?! A close family member was the baby's father. Through some crazy circumstances, one day, she was pregnant and had no idea how.

In fact, it was months before she was convinced that she was pregnant. I know this seems wild, but if you've been in the throes of foster care, not much should surprise you anymore. I was skeptical about her situation until the first night, when her baby woke up in the middle of the night screaming. Gina slept right through it, one foot from the baby's crib.

Thus began months of me getting up in the middle of the night to care for my baby, and again to care for hers (by waking her up and helping her mother her own child). She had zero maternal instincts. Zero.

And her baby, the result of a couple generations of incest, had an internal cleft pallet, clubbed feet, poor vision, and by the end of her time with us, had begun having seizures. Gina and her baby had to move to a medically fragile home. Gina took us through the wringer... graffiti in our bathroom, lying about us to our friends and acquaintances, stealing from us, hoarding food, and treating her baby as more of a dress-up doll than a living human being.

Gina's mother relied on Gina to read all of the court documents and papers for her. Her mother truly loved her, but lacked the resources and maturity in herself to be able to care for her daughter. We love Gina and have always kept our home open to her.

Over the years, she has stayed in touch, though her life is less than we hope for her. She reconnected with her family members. She birthed a second child (after losing her first to foster care). She got involved with drugs, gangs, and guns, all of which she has posted openly on Facebook.

In the last month that we had Gina, Michael's older sister moved in. She was fifteen and had been in the system long enough to know how to work it. They wouldn't move her when she asked... so she pulled the strings she'd learned to pull, and got her way, moving in with us.

In that month, she realized that the ways she'd fantasized our home being easier or better were false. She imagined that because we didn't know her as well, she'd be able to get away with everything. However, she couldn't get away with anything for very long. We found the condoms in her bag, the ones she claimed she was holding for her friend, while she preached abstinence to her brothers. We caught her lies, her theft, her manipulation, and she couldn't stand it. She decided she wanted to move back in with her previous foster mother, and we all felt it was a good idea. We let her make that choice, but told her our home was always open to her.

She stayed in foster care a couple more years before running away for good. She had often lectured her brothers on how good they had it. On how much more they were loved and cared for than they'd been in their bio home. She had memories of it, while they didn't.

Yet, in the end, she couldn't abide by any of the things she coached them in. She died at the age of nineteen. She was eight months pregnant. I heard that she'd had so many abortions that the clinic wouldn't let her have anymore... thus the pregnancy. She was living with her boyfriend. After she'd run, she tried to come back to foster care on her own, but just couldn't live under the authority of adults and eventually ran again. The initial report said she'd had a seizure, fallen, and broken her nose on the way down, somehow dying. The speculation, however, was domestic violence leading to her accidental death. Tragic.

We also took in Michael's two little brothers for a month. Because of a certification issue in their foster home, they needed a place to stay.

We love these boys.

By then, Michael had been with us about a year. His primary hope for many months had been reuniting with his brothers. He loved them deeply and felt responsible to take care of them. He still saw them at school for a while, but he really longed to live with them.

We had the chance, and all three boys were together under our roof. However, having lived for so long without a father, good or bad, they were desperate for that male attention. My husband lavished it. When we asked Michael how he liked having his two little brothers live with us, he said, "I like it better when they just visit." In the last eight years, they've been caught in the horrors of red tape, bureaucracy, and an egotistical social worker (more to come on that in a chapter 3). The two brothers are now separated. We understand that one is in a group home, the other is still in foster care. We've heard there are drug and gang activities as well.

Nineteen months after the birth of our firstborn, I was about to birth our third child (I'd miscarried our second). At the same time, Jeremy had parent-teacher conferences for his class. One foster parent came in and told him, "I want you to know that Jillian (his third grade student) will be moving sometime this year. I have too many kids and I can't keep her." They ended the conference with my husband saying that, worst case scenario, he was a certified foster parent and could possibly take her.

We got a phone call.

"We would like you to take Jillian into your home," the Social Worker said, "However we don't want to keep moving her around. We only want to move her into an adoptive placement. Will you commit to adopting her?"

I had never even met her, except in the way that I'd met every one of Jeremy's students… when I'd walk in and smile and they'd all say, "Hello, Mrs. Pusey."

Okay, they can't actually make you adopt a kid. But being people of our word, we wanted to honor their request and took it seriously.

We decided to go for it. Jillian had been Jeremy's student in second and third grade. He knew her well enough to know that she would be a good fit for our home. We asked Michael what he thought of bringing Jillian into our family (he knew her from school), and he was onboard. He was ready to have a playmate-sibling his own age. She moved in exactly one month before our baby was born.

We'd parented nine children in twenty months.

When we began fostering, we really didn't know anyone else doing it. As we attended trainings with our foster agency, we began to meet people who had been in the trenches, some for many years. Others were newbies like us. While we were welcomed by our faith community, there were lots of learning curves for all of us. For example, what happens when bio family show up at church and want to see the kids?

However, as people watched our journey, many began to envision it for themselves. Others had simultaneously been on their own journeys and eventually joined us. As of today, we have over forty families in our circle who have either adopted or fostered. More are currently getting certified. Having this community of people to walk alongside us at various stages has been a living breath of fresh air.

Literally.

And you know it... you know those times you've met someone, maybe a total stranger, but when you start sharing stories about foster care or adoption, it's like you can breathe again. Someone gets it. And they're not judging you. They're not telling you how typical your kids are. Or applauding how amazing you are to do this. You've met another soldier in the trenches, and you may have nothing else in common, but this is enough.

There you have it, our imperfectly beautiful family, our hard experiences, some past, some current. All reflect a persistent hope that we can be part of a solution in this world for the tragedy of foster care, orphanages, and sometimes our own hurts and pain.

Are you ready? We're about to jump into the greatest challenge that foster and adoptive parents face. We're not going to vent and focus on the negative; we are going to seek the beauty in the mess together. We are going to search out hope. We are going to remind ourselves why we do this parenting-strangers thing. And we are going to acknowledge out loud in the open that this is hard work.

If you're tired of pretending you've got it all together or that you've got the perfect kids or that this is always easy, if you sometimes wonder if you've made a mistake, if you find yourself beaten down the by the judgments of others or yourself, if you feel the strain of raising adoptive and foster kids on your marriage or on your own health, then keep reading.

Together we are going to name these challenges, acknowledge that they exist, that they are hard, and that, at the end of the day, there is still hope.

CHAPTER 2

The Challenge of Beginning

"Our children were harmed in & through relationships, & they will find healing in & through nurturing relationships."

—Dr. Karyn Purvis,
co-author of The Connected Child

Of all of the challenges we deal with in fostering and adopting children, this is the one that sets all of the rest in motion.

The waiting.

Waiting is hard. Torturous, even. Whether you are a foster parent, adopt privately, or adopt internationally, waiting is your introduction to this new life you've been planning. It takes a great deal of time and energy to seek out agencies, applications, interviews, choose your child (or accept the placement), and sign your name on a million dotted lines.

We walk through the flurry of to-do's, marking off each task as it's completed. We hand over our due diligence to the authorities.

And then nothing happens.

You've read about all of the need. You've seen the photos. Read the articles.

If there are so many kids who need homes, why does it take so long to get one?

There are many reasons, of course, but I believe the largest one leads into the next chapter: The Challenge of a Broken System. International adoptions deal with visas and national rules that seem to change at a moment's notice. You have to deal with at least two countries, each with a roll of red tape and an agency that helps mediate the adoption with their own roll of tape.

Then there's waiting to be chosen. Waiting for the family that is releasing their child to go through all of the sales-pitched binders of each family and choose one. To choose you. To see in your album the very thing they are looking for in a family for their son or daughter.

The waiting is agonizing. It's silent and yet so loud, isn't it? It seems to scream into the silence, "You won't be good enough! No one will want you! See? The phone isn't ringing because THIS IS A DEAD END. You'll be an awful parent, and everyone knows it."

Ouch

To borrow a phrase from Anne Lammott's "Bird by Bird," put that voice in the jar where it belongs. Pick it up by its mouse tail and put the lid on. The silence of waiting seems to release the whole zoo into your brain, to scream and shout in all of its dissonance, a racket so loud it's hard to remember to dream. To believe. To anticipate. Because the fears already begin to overwhelm.

If you're not waiting to be chosen, then you're waiting to get that first placement. Or to get the call that the birth mother went into labor and you should go to the hospital to meet your baby. It all takes so long. And it never makes sense. There's just really no good explanation, except for the reason I'll come back to over and over.

Governments can't raise kids. Systems can't either. They both suck at it big time.

In California, we have to wait six months to begin the adoption process with a foster child. These six months can seem like a prison-sentence except the torture is all mental and still, somehow, so time-consuming.

We knew with our first child that, even though he was only supposed to stay for the weekend, we'd keep him forever if they'd let us. Now he's our oldest child. It took a year and a half from his first day in our home until his adoption finalized. Five hundred and forty-eight days! His parents were already deemed unfit for many unfortunate reasons.

And in that year and a half, we had to get a court order to give him medicine, get the agency's permission to take him to my parents' house, forty-five minutes away. We spent days getting him a passport, which we'd heard was impossible, just so we could take him on a trip with us. We had to give an eight-year-old TWENTY DOLLARS A MONTH, regardless of whether or not he ever lifted a finger to help around the house, whether he ran away for twenty-seven days of the month, or whatever. Period.

When our foster daughter needed surgery, we had to get a court order. We wanted to move our foster son from the school where he was being bullied to my husband's school. More paperwork, more permissions, more judges.

That year and a half felt like being chained to the walls of a crazy house. With clowns juggling balls of fire and cackling creepy laughs. All we wanted was to take care of this child… and it was so hard, irritating even.

Until his adoption.

We were finally FREE! Free to travel, free to visit grandparents without alerting the county, free to go to the beach without alerting the county, free to go sledding without alerting the county, free to NOT visit people we didn't want to visit. The list goes on. And for those of you who've foster-adopted, you know what I mean. Especially when you have a wait period. You want to do the best for this child, but you can't. Your hands are tied because all of the government officials, who don't live in your house, need to sign all of the paperwork for every single movement of that child. It's excruciating.

Yet, I believe it's a strange sort of practice for everything that's coming. It develops character. Perseverance. It solidifies our vision and purpose. I understand the six-month wait, they have to consider the "honeymoon" and the drastic decisions people can make while on that love-high. Many families (even with the wait) have found themselves on the other side of adoption, thinking, *maybe we should have taken more time to get to know each other first.*

Practical reasons aside, I believe that some of our best growth as humans happens in that waiting.

We are forced to confront so many aspects of ourselves: our impatience, our fears, our anger, and our own hurts. In this space, we often finally make peace with ourselves for who we are. The waiting is our emotional battleground. We duke it out with all of our negative self-thoughts, our fears of what might (or might not) happen, and who we are in the midst of all of it. WHO ARE WE as a person if we aren't given this child? Or as a person if we are? Am I looking for my own healing in this little person? Or am I looking to heal them? Because really, neither will happen, not in the adoption, and, at least, not in the ways you'd expect.

So we take to the mat of "waiting" and meet our ugly selves. The selves who demand, who grumble, who complain, who get irritated and short with people. The selves who shake in fear so that our nightmares fill our vision during the day, because we don't want to get hurt. Not again. But as we wrestle with our ugly selves, we eventually find our beautiful self. The self who persevered through this crazy adventure of reaching for our children, crossing all barriers, raising funds we never thought we could raise, dealt with the most difficult people, until finally... FINALLY, the day comes.

Because, even in all of the waiting, when it happens, it's BAM! You have a kid!

And sometimes, it's in THAT moment, that you understand the timing. Understand why it needed to be this way. Hopefully, you'll realize it was everything you needed for what was to come in loving this child.

Some of us will never understand the timing.

But there is a reason, a bigger and better one than just that governments suck at raising kids and finding them homes.

Spend this time WELL.

If you're in this season of waiting, pass the time productively. You're not alone. For those of us further on the path, those days, months, and years seem like such a blip in the midst of all of the life that follows. Where life feels on hold for you now, it will feel like a flash flood soon enough. Don't spend this time agonizing. Read blogs of other adoptive/foster families, find the best books on raising adopted children, watch YouTube videos, connect with the stories of others.

Christine Moers is one of my favorite parents to watch on YouTube.[1] She has five children, a blend of adopted and birthed, and all have a special need of some kind. She makes me feel so normal. I think you'll love her too. You will be inspired and invigorated. Okay, sometimes, also terrified, but keep reading.

Begin to form community

I can't say this enough. Having a solid community of people around you who "get it" will be among your greatest lifesavers later. START NOW. Don't wait. Find an adoption group on Facebook in your area. GO to monthly picnics. Listen to their stories and share yours. You're only in the beginning stage, but it's a good one! And they'll reminisce that time in their story and you'll see, over and over, that the waiting truly does end. You'll see families a couple steps ahead of you doing it. It's possible. It happens. There is light at the end of the very long tunnel of beginning your adoption story.

Dream!

Don't stop dreaming. Your journey may have curves in the road that you didn't expect. You may end up in a different country. You may end up with a different gender. You may end up with a different child. But your adoption journey will be your journey and no one else's. Keep dreaming. Keep believing. If this has been a cry of your heart, then follow that cry. Don't let the discouragements of waiting dim your hope. Print that photo (or bunches of them) and hang them everywhere. Or find a quote or verse that gives you hope and inspiration; write it on your mirrors, on sticky notes, in your car. Keep your vision and hope before you.

In the next few chapters, we are going to dive into the challenges of a broken system, a system that keeps us waiting, that requires so much advocacy, managing the red tape, navigating misleading information, and dealing with the disrespect and neglect we often face as the foster and adoptive parent.

Sounds like fun, right? This is a biggie and you don't want to miss it. If you're just beginning, the next chapter will give you a step up from the rest of us who figured it out along the way. For the rest of us, the following chapters are that breath of fresh air after a much-needed rain... they'll wrap you up and say, "You're okay; it's not you... it's them." And the warm fuzzies will creep up in your soul, and you'll sigh, thinking, *I sure hoped so.*

Let's do this.

1. Christine Moers, "Welcome to My Brain" (blog), accessed October 8, 2015, www.welcometomybrain.net/p/about.html

CHAPTER 3

❧

The Challenge of the System

❧

"It is the children the world often breaks who grow up to save it."

—Frank Warren, author of PostSecret

The challenge of the broken system is among the most challenging on the list. Some of my survey participants said they could handle everything else: the awkward social behavior of their children, the advocacy for medical services, dealing with the biological family, the endless waiting, but dealing with the system was nearly their undoing. I'd be surprised if there's one person out there who didn't run into kinks, glitches, and seemingly unnecessary bureaucracy in the pursuit of their children.

I realize that, in the midst of the broken system, the cracks and crevices, the endless files, the burned-out social workers, that there is much good. I will acknowledge those.

But there is also a lot that is devastatingly hard in trying to love and parent children from within the System, whether that's a local county, an adoption agency, orphanages, or even a personal foster agency.

By *System*, I refer to the institutions that keep foster care and adoption possible: the social workers, attorneys, judges, agencies, the laws, and enforcers of the laws. All were created to meet the intensely growing need of social orphans and orphans. But it wasn't always this way.

In 1853, Charles Loring Brace, an American minister, took his faith outside of the church building and into the streets of New York City. In his book, The *Orphan Trains*, Stephen O'Connor wrote, "In 1849, New York's first police chief reported that 3,000 children or close to one percent of the city's total population—lived on the streets and had no place to sleep but in alleys and abandoned buildings or under stairways. At first, the authorities had dealt with these vagrant children mainly by incarcerating them in adult prisons and almshouses and then, beginning in the 1820s, by building juvenile prisons and asylums, which were barely less harsh or punitive."

Charles believed in prevention and spent much of his energy beginning kindergartens, offering free dental clinics, job placement training, training programs, reading rooms, and lodging houses for boys (think Newsies and "street rats"). He also began the Orphan Train movement, where he found Christian families across the United States who would take in these children. Thus, he is considered the "Father of modern foster care."

His idea of organizing care for orphans was radical, but also quickly popular. Brace believed that helping the city's orphans become productive members of society could be accomplished through work skills, education, and a healthy family atmosphere. When he and some like-minded friends formed the Children's Aid Society, states began copying his efforts; thus, foster care spread throughout the nation.

As with anything, I imagine, once it becomes a government initiative, you may have the benefit of some funding, but the rest is red tape, bureaucracy, and a business-mentality instead of genuine, calling-driven aid. The humanitarian heart for the poor that drove Charles Brace couldn't be replicated in government institutions.

Governments were never meant to raise children. They can't do it.

I'll pause here to say that I do NOT believe that every person should or can foster or adopt. This road is NOT for everyone. There was a day when I said differently. The false message that many agencies send out involves a warm welcome and call to everyone to foster and adopt.

The fliers, posters, and Internet ads and videos present a beautifully blended family, full of smiles, of hope and promise, of the honor and nobility of rescuing a child. They are designed to grab the heart of every person to be a part of this beautiful family image. Right now, google "Foster Family" and click on images. You'll see picture after picture of happy, smiling, perfect families.

If they showed the true image of what life raising these kids is often like, very few would sign up. No one is posting pictures of the teen-sized tantrums with holes punched or kicked in walls, the poop smeared on the wall, you banging your head against the wall (figuratively or otherwise), and the child screaming, "I hate you!" Yeah, we can all smile for the camera, too... but it doesn't capture the days of passive aggressive silence, the agony of waiting, of loving, of leaving.

They have a hard enough time getting people to certify as it is.

I worked in Social Services in the same county of our adoptions. I learned that the county was certifying the homes of Southeast Asian migrant workers who spoke no English. The workers were told that if they could provide meals and shelter for children, they could make decent money (compared to their below-poverty wages earned working the fields all day).

The county had so few homes in which to place foster children that they were utilizing the homes of these migrant workers. These kids were being torn away from their families and placed in a house where the adults couldn't even speak their language! There was little nurturing, no ability to be involved with school, no real education to help with medical issues that might arise... and this was okay. Because they believed they had no other options. Talk about traumatizing a traumatized child.

The system is faulty and shouldn't be raising kids.

And when we decide to foster or adopt locally, we enter into an agreement with this broken system. We pick up the pieces of the additional trauma it causes. This is not part of the training you'll hear in most county offices during your orientation.

No, they leave us to blame everything on the biological families. Does it matter where the hurt comes from? Yes and no... hurt is hurt and these kids come to us from a seat of loss from the moment they arrive, no matter how long or little they've been in the system.

But I think it's wise for us to consider the additional trauma that our kids have experienced being passed around as they have, being told over and over again in so many words, "You aren't good enough to keep; on you go," or "I have too many of you, so you'll need a new home."

Some of you have shared stories of travesties within the System. That could be a whole book on its own, all of the ways the system fails. BUT it's all that we have to work with. And within it are people who truly care and who are trying to work within the fragments to bring about some good. Let's not forget them, the people who raised their voices in advocacy for us.

We had an incorrigible county worker once. She was so difficult to work with and kind of clueless about how much so. But, since we were with a Foster Family Agency (FFA), we utilized our agency worker. We invited him to be mediator between us and, essentially, the System. For a time, we set a boundary that we would not speak directly with the county worker (because it caused so much more stress than necessary) and would relay all things through him. This was unusual, but I was spent trying to raise this kid, let alone deal with his county worker.

Our agency worker graciously complied, and, though he might not have agreed with our approach, he stepped sacrificially in as our buffer. It was exactly what we needed for that time. When the adoptions finalized, we were genuinely able to hug our county worker and express gratitude for her work, simply because we had someone willing to step in and cushion us while we took some time to breathe and learn our rights.

Michael's two little brothers (mentioned in the last chapter) went on to other foster homes. At one point, their bio family abducted them. The kids returned with gaping emotional wounds. These boys had been making slow but steady progress in their foster home with the single mother. When they returned to her, they were out of control behaviorally. So much so, that even though she loved them deeply, she didn't feel she could meet their needs. She agreed to keep them until they could find a new foster placement.

The FFA found the perfect home for them (in my opinion). They were an ethnic match, a family with high values and morals, and wanted both boys. Everything checked out. I was beside-myself-thrilled. I'd always felt guilty for not adopting them. At the same time, I knew I had met my limit in the kids we had and it wouldn't have been the best option for them. "I can't save everyone," I had to tell myself.

Well, the county worker wouldn't move them to this perfect adoptive family. Why? Because SHE hadn't found the family. She refused to take any families that the FFA found. Her ego trip led to the devastation of these boys. The youngest is still in foster care. As of this writing, he's about fourteen and involved in gangs and drugs and who knows what else.

He's on the same destructive path as his biological family before him, but this time I blame it on that ridiculous county worker who couldn't get over her own power trip, sentencing these boys to much less than what they could've had. We continue to hope for the best.

As I mentioned in Chapter 1, Gina's baby had a gamut of health needs and eventually needed to be placed in a medically fragile home. I sat in on the big team meeting where everyone made decisions for this small family. I advocated, sadly, for separating mother and baby to give them both a chance.

They did not take my advice and moved mother and baby to another home. Once in that home, the new foster family took the mother on a vacation, leaving the care of the baby in a medically fragile respite home. In those days apart, the baby flourished. She began to develop in ways and at rates no one had ever seen from her.

As soon as mom entered the picture again, baby regressed drastically and immediately. The new foster parents reported their observations to the workers and eventually, mother and baby went their own ways. Baby lives with a good friend of mine. She is eight now. She's been on her deathbed more times than I can count on both hands but keeps pulling out of it. She laughs. She has a handful of words. And she lives with a lot of pain and pain management.

But she is loved deeply, desperately, radically.

Her adoptive mother has sacrificed more than anyone knows for the care of this child. She has advocated life or death situations for this child relentlessly. I'm convinced this baby is alive today because she was adopted.

Meanwhile, birth mother is lost. She doesn't go to school, doesn't work, and whittles away her day in a constant high with a new child by her side in all-inclusive enabled living. She gets welfare, county services, and other government aid.

Our system is truly broken.

We may have known it and we may not, but this is the monster's mouth we dove into when we chose to foster or adopt. Even if your adoption story was international, *you've got stories!* Stories of lost paperwork, of misinformation about your child, of scummy agencies that were prepared to hand you someone entirely different than who you had flown across the world to receive.

Forget the kids for a moment, navigating the red tape and bureaucracy and the government trying to do our job is HARD WORK. This is part of what we signed up for. It's part of why we wanted to adopt our kids so quickly, to rescue them and get them out of the System's teeth. Social Services is trying to do a job it was never intended to do. The purpose is noble but the result is horrifying.

It's okay to not want to talk to your social worker anymore.

It's okay to be infuriated with the amount of educating and advocacy you have to do for a hurting child within the System. It's okay to feel broken over the experiences you've had, trying to love a child.

Well, it's not okay. It shouldn't be like this.

But it is like this... so you experiencing it is normal. It's brave what you've done. Even if you didn't realize the amount of courage you'd need to walk this road, you're doing it. Your courage is rising up. That anger is being used for good.

You care.

And some days, we need to be reminded that we care, don't we? Sometimes, I'm sure that all my caring has dried up, and I need someone to point out the ways that they see it.

And in you, I see it.

I see that you still care.

Or this wouldn't be so hard.

Thank you. Thank you for braving this system. Thank you for being Marios or Luigis, hopping down the dungeons of Social Services, pounding the head of the Big Boss, so you can give these kids a chance to have family. So that you can give yourself a chance to see what you're made of.

It's pure gold, friend.

Let's walk this journey together. In the next few chapters, we'll talk about social worker turnaround, dealing with the disrespect we face as foster and adoptive parents, the need for our advocacy within the system, the red tape and bureaucracy that halts nearly every step, and the misleading info that changes everything.

We're going to be people who overcome this system, championing the rights of our families, and searching out the gems hidden in the cracks of the System. There are gems, friends!

Let's go find them.

CHAPTER 4

The Challenge of High Turnaround Rates of Social Workers

"Social work is a Band-Aid on the festering wounds of society."

—Chase Alexander, journalist and editor

The turnaround rate of social workers is one of the great tragedies of the broken System. It not only causes the hardest challenges but is also the result of the hardest challenges. These people became social workers because they love people. They care for people. They wanted to be on the front lines of helping people.

I know because I was one of them.

My undergraduate degree is social work. I shared their hope, their vision, and their purpose.

Today, our counties and agencies are full of individuals who originally sought to help people but found themselves in a quagmire of tape and up to their necks in paperwork, with hardly any time or energy to see the people they once dreamed of helping.

We find ourselves caught in their same quagmire. However, often, by the time we get there, they're on the brink of a nervous breakdown and career-identity crisis. They are dealing with the disillusionment of all the purpose they imagined their job would hold.

Then we walk in the door, and they can't remember our name, let alone that they were supposed to sign that court document and send it by yesterday, or that you've already turned IN your dossier and... where the heck did they put it? Or that, once again, your child threw up all of the Cheetos and Coke on the way home from their visit with mom, and can we please stop these insane visits?

And then, they just quit. No notice. Just one day, you call and it's not Jennifer anymore; it's Susan, and who are you again? And what were we working on? And "I'll get back to you next week," which means never, unless you call every single day until you're dead.

I left multiple phone messages on the voicemail of an Adoption Assistance Program social worker who had quit (but I had no idea because she still had a functioning voicemail). No one was checking her messages and no one was forwarding them on to the new worker. So when I finally got a hold of an outpatient service in Florida to help with my son, the new worker was completely blind-sided by how desperate our post-adopt situation was. She had no paper trail of our multiple attempts at getting him (and us) help. Within a few months of working all that out, that worker left and we had another new one.

We have to start over each time.

Social workers are burned out, overworked, and can't know the details of all of their cases. The Child Welfare League of America (CWLA) recommends that social workers have twelve to fifteen children on their caseload, and while the number varies, many social workers are dealing with four to six times that number.

Burnout is a serious epidemic among our social service workers. According to Segal, Smith, Segal, and Robinson, "Burnout is a state of emotional, mental, and physical exhaustion caused by excessive and prolonged stress. It occurs when you feel overwhelmed and unable to meet constant demands. As the stress continues, you begin to lose the interest or motivation that led you to take on a certain role in the first place. Burnout reduces your productivity and saps your energy, leaving you feeling increasingly helpless, hopeless, cynical, and resentful. Eventually, you may feel like you have nothing more to give."[1]

Right? It's not just social workers dealing with burnout. I'm going to guess anyone reading this who has foster or adoptive children has experienced these same symptoms... except quitting our job isn't a viable option.

In addition to burnout, social workers often deal with compassion fatigue. In his article, "Secondary Trauma and Foster Parents: Understanding Its Impact and Taking Steps to Protect Them," David Conrad wrote, "It is the stress resulting from helping or wanting to help a traumatized or suffering person."[2] This leads to a gradual lessening of compassion over time, which I speak more about in Chapter 24.

We can understand why there is so much turnaround in social services. Men and women who entered the field to change the world for good are overworked, overstressed, and disillusioned. They quit and the next starryeyed dreamer takes their place.

I know.

I've worked in social services for a long time.

I started out the same starryeyed graduate, looking for the "big" job with the county, the one where I could really dig my feet in and be the change.

Then I watched one friend after another, whose eyes turn glazed and become frustrated, hopeless, and done trying to help a broken system.

So I went the private foster agency route, both in work and in adoption.

This made a world of difference.

But even though we can understand the reason for the rapid turnaround, it's still one of the most frustrating aspects of entering the system as a parent.

In some cases, it's as bad as what Benjamin and Mary shared: *"We had one of our daughter's since she was two days old. Parental rights were terminated when she was about a year old. There wasn't any family to speak of; the judge wanted her to stay with us. We waited a year and half for our caseworker to redact the files and get the paperwork in order. Talk about wasted resources and living in limbo. When I reached my breaking point and complained, I was told to stop making waves or they would move her. It scared us! We hired a lawyer, sued CPS to become her managing conservators, and then consented to our own adoption. The downside was that she lost subsidy. And we spent* *nearly $8,000 in legal fees."*

Dealing with social worker turnaround is beyond frustrating. It sets us back, delays already slow progress, and makes us want to yell and cry. For some of us, like Benjamin and Mary, complaining had dire consequences.

Yet behind it all, there are real people who started this job wanting to help others. Along the way, they realize how broken the system is that hired them and how disillusioned they've become. They are overworked, underpaid, and exhausted. Naturally, they lose interest in their work as they also lose vision, compassion, and purpose.

We get caught right up in that with them. We deal with their aftermath. We suffer their growing apathy. We start over and over again.

Who else is willing to do this for our kids? If we don't push through, who will? If everyone around us gives up, who's left but us?

We, the brave and bold and weary and committed and confused. We keep on.

You and I, we're in this together. And together, we can do it. You might feel like the only sane person in your circle... but you are not alone.

Love Your Social Worker

You may not feel the fuzzy-wuzzies for them. They may be the bane of your fostering and adopting experience. But I'm a firm believer in "killing with kindness." I'll be the first to admit that in the midst of a frustrating conversation, choosing to love is NOT on the forefront of my mind. I have to take a deep breath and remind myself that this is a person and that this person has a story.

I have no idea what *difficulties* are going on in their lives. I have no idea what they've had to deal with that day. I don't know the pressures weighing them down from supervisors. I don't know about their family lives. But I know that they want to help people. I don't need to be one more reason they hate their job. So, I bite my tongue, choke down the less-than-helpful ways I want to say things, whisper a prayer, smile, and nod. The helpful things I'll try to say in kindness and compassion. I'll try to hope for the best. And when they come to our door, or call our house, or send that email, they will be met with truth, yes, but truth that tries to empower them to be their best in a hard situation. Does this sound exhausting? It is. But it's also really good practice for the kids we're raising.

Find a Healthy Venting Place

I'm not calling for a negativity bash. Negativity breeds more negativity. I *am* saying that you need a place to go to process all of the frustrations that you are dealing with in the process. Maybe that's an adoption group. Maybe that's a friend who is fostering or adopting along with you. Maybe it's a mentor or coach or counselor. Maybe writing in a journal is good enough for you.

Find a place where you can say all of the ugly things without the backlash of damaging the relationships that you need intact within the System. Find someone who won't pull you down with more negativity, but who will listen, listen, and listen some more. Ideally, find a person who sees the good in every situation. These people often have a good point. If we let them, they can pull us out of the muck of negativity and despair, and remind us that there is good in everything.

They can remind us that this could be worse. And it could.

In the next chapter, we are going to look at how the System sometimes bullies us, devaluing our role in their program. We'll talk about how to make our voices matter and to demand the respect we deserve, not because we are so special, but because our kids are. Disrespecting our influence in our children's lives, as well as the information we've gleaned living with them, is a grave mistake.

Our partnership with the broken System is crucial and we can't give up.

1. Jeanne Segal, Melinda Smith, Robert Segal, and Lawrence Robinson, "Stress Symptoms, Signs, and Causes: Understanding Stress, Its Harmful Effects, and the Best Ways to Cope," HelpGuide.org, last updated September 2015, accessed October 9, 2015, www.helpguide.org/articles/stress/stress-symptoms-causes-and-effects.htm

2. David Conrad, "Secondary Trauma and Foster Parents: Understanding Its Impact and Taking Steps to Protect Them," National Child Welfare Resource Center for Organizational Improvement, accessed October 9, 2015, www.nrcoi.org/rcpdfs/Sec.Trauma-foster.pdf

CHAPTER 5

The Challenge of Making Our Voices Heard

"You may encounter many defeats, but you must not be defeated. In fact, it may be necessary to encounter the defeats, so you can know who you are, what you can rise from, how you can still come out of it."

—Maya Angelou

The high stress; the emotional, mental, and physical exhaustion; and the inability to meet the constant demands placed on employees of the System leads to a culture of disregard for parents. Though we have been gracious, willing, and committed to join them in taking care of these kids, we are often devalued and undermined.

Our voice matters.

But that's not usually what we hear from the System. We aren't informed about meetings, and if we are, our opinion holds little weight. The kids know they can threaten us by calling their attorney or social worker, and depending on who they are and how they view our role, that can be a scary thing or a really great idea!

Because of the positions I've held (Facilitator, Case Manager, Support Counselor for Intensive Treatment Foster Care (ITFC), and others) I have spent a great deal of time in meetings with social workers, lawyers, and the plethora of other job positions and titles that participate in the team meetings for one child. I have sat in the seat of the "qualified" because of my degree and title. While I'm a firm believer that experience is often as valuable (if not more) than a piece of paper, when it's necessary, I pull the degree card.

Because I have to.

Because I have no voice if I don't flash my "I'm qualified to be heard and considered" card.

This is true for any parent who is a member of that team. The team might try to give the parent a voice, but often the language used is System-language and considered "over their heads." The parent is asked for input, at times, but then decisions are made regardless.

Yet we parents are the ones who know these kids. We know what they need. We know their challenges and struggles. We live with their challenges and struggles EVERY DAY. We are in the school meetings. We are in the doctor's office. We are at the kitchen table and the bedroom door and the driver's seat.

But we have the smallest voice in the System.

Unless you have some qualification.

I have used my qualifications to help countless parents. I sit beside them and demand their voice be heard. Our voice. I keep bringing their points up again and again until they are part of the solution. I say the obvious things that seem irrelevant to the decision makers.

And this is sad.

Because really… I'm just another mama trying to give this adoption story a happy ending. I know better. My voice is no more valuable. But I have the card, and sometimes my friends don't.

We are educated, and not because we've been to school and ticked off the necessary boxes to get our piece of paper. We've been in the trenches. We live in the trenches. And we have a right to be heard. Not just a right but a duty… it's to everyone's benefit. It serves the common goal of truly doing what's best for the child.

One article, "Meeting the Challenges of Contemporary Foster Care" by Chipungu and Bent-Goodley, noted that despite provisions in the federal law, one-third of caregivers in a California study had not received any written notices about court hearings regarding children in their care.

Yet, when properly notified, these parents attended the court proceedings. The same study found that social workers, attorneys, and judges were either ambivalent or opposed to foster parents being involved in court hearings and having a say in decisions made for the kids in their care.[1] What is this craziness?

They don't want us in the courtroom, in their planning meetings, and part of the decision-making process because they don't respect our experience. Friends affirmed how hard it is to try to be a help and a resource to a System that constantly says, "Who are you? Step back, please."

Sometimes, if we judge by actions, it seems the System's goal is to return a child to their nuclear family regardless of the well-being of the child. Sometimes, the goal seems to be to make the child feel as in-control of their life situation as possible. Sometimes, the goal seems to be spoiling the child with rights and privileges to make up for their shoddy start in life. All at the expense of what's actually good for them.

There are times when returning the child to their nuclear family *is* in the best interest of everyone.

But not always.

The System has sent too many kids back into a tragedy where we, from the distant sidelines, watch knowingly as the child and family spiral into another traumatic incident that either lands the child back into the system, more damaged than before, or dead.

But we don't have to stand by silently and watch the tragedy.

Speak Up

Our voices matter. Does that mean we stand on the table and demand their attention? No. But if we're able, we make sure they hear us. We ask good questions. We inform ourselves so we can speak intelligently about the issues being discussed. We present ourselves, not as timid victims, but as the guests of honor. I know this is awkward and perhaps intimidating. I'm an introvert, and if you're like me, this is out of your comfort zone. But so is parenting these kids. Find your voice and use it. And if this terrifies you, bring a friend! I've been an advocate for families. I still offer to advocate in school meetings for friends or even just to show up and be a team-player.

Sometimes, having someone beside you who CAN speak up, who knows the situation, or who has a fancy "card" they can pull is enough to help you find your voice too. It's helpful to walk into a room full of "important" strangers and know that you have a friend. I've met some really great social workers, case workers, and court-appointed special advocates (CASA) who do this for their people. One day, you may be able to do this for others, too.

Persistence

Isn't this what truly drives us? Exhausted, defeated, and frustrated, we keep on fighting nonetheless. We keep speaking up. We keep knocking on the door. Because this is our love. I believe true love is messy. It shows up in the least expected places. It is tested and refined over and over. We practice the art of love every time we KEEP ON.

Don't give up. I know that's easy to say, believe me. There have been days when, with tears in my eyes, I was sure we made the biggest mistake ever and I had nothing left to give. I was depleted. My husband would remind me of the life-grabbing words of a friend: "You brought these kids into your home. That is enough." And every day, with a fresh start, we try again and we keep on pressing in.

Being a parent in a room full of professional people who talk over you, smile condescendingly when you share, and respond on surveys that they don't want you there, is intimidating. It's frustrating. We know what we can offer but it's not always welcome. Sometimes, the ego-trip of having a degree or job title is enough to silence the true expert in the room: you.

I know this isn't every situation and every meeting. I've known lovely social workers who take it upon themselves to make sure the parent is heard and respected. THANK THOSE PEOPLE! It's a huge challenge learning to parent these kids, but to feel that the people in the System are against us is deflating. It can make us feel helpless.

But we don't have to feel helpless. We can find our voice. We will persist in love. We will speak up. We will commit to doing what's best for our kids, regardless of how we're treated.

Because this is the art of love.

Because we are sometimes their only advocate, which is what we talk about in the next chapter. We didn't realize when we adopted or fostered that we were also signing up to be an advocate. A change agent. Until we found ourselves in the throes of fighting for this kid, for their medical needs, their educational needs, their rights. We fight them at home, and we fight the System for them the rest of the time.

Our lives mingling with theirs is a constant use of our ability to speak up, speak out, and defend the vulnerable. This is true regardless of international adoption, local adoption, or foster care. It seems that *forever* we will be in meetings discussing the best interest of our children. And if not for our own kids, then for those of others because of our experiences. The next chapter will speak to all of the ways we take on advocacy, sometimes against our will, in order to provide the best for our kids.

---

1. Sandra Stukes Chipungu and Tricia B. Bent-Goodley, "Meeting the Challenges of Contemporary Foster Care," Children, Families, and Foster Care 14, no. 1 (Winter 2004): 1, accessed October 9, 2015, www.princeton.edu/futureofchildren/publications/journals/article/index.xml?journalid=40&articleid=135&sectionid=888

CHAPTER 6

❦❧

The Challenge
of Being an Advocate

❦❧

*"The art of love is largely the
art of persistence."*

—Albert Ellis

With a system as broken, misleading, and burned out as ours, we find ourselves in the role of advocate time and again.

Did you have any idea how much you'd have to know? To speak up about? To be bold with?

We didn't. And neither did our friends, Robert and Melissa. One of their greatest challenges is *"the HUGE amount of advocacy that is required. Caring for all Brenton's needs are easy compared to the advocacy for his supplies and managing all his doctors. Then much of the advocacy is due to technical issues: you have to follow up on everything because you never know when your case got buried, the fax didn't go through, the computer screwed up, the worker went on leave, or the agency had to hire all new employees and they are being trained still. Lots of grace is needed and lots of follow up."*

Whether we are introverted or extroverted, this job of fostering and adopting requires endless hours of informing ourselves, informing others, and standing firm in what's right for our kids and our families. It's like beating back the waves of the ocean with a broom. It's often daunting and seems hopeless. It's enough trying to raise these kids and not lose our minds sometimes... but this?

And as much as we hate it, it's necessary. I know we each have stories of ways our persistence in a cause has won a victory in the life of our child.

We have to be their advocate in their educational spheres, in the doctor's office, in the psychiatrist's office, and in the social worker's office. We have to demand our rights often in a system bent on giving all of the power to the children (upon whom it's unfair to place such large expectations) or to biological family members.

One of our foster children had a biological sister with whom she had little contact. One day, our foster child attended a summer youth event where she met the friend of her sister. No big deal, right? Except that this friend snapped a photo of my child and sent it to her sister.

Which is how we learned that the biological sister had some serious issues of her own.

A few days later, while the kids were at school, I received a phone call from our FFA social worker. "Do you know where your child is?" he asked.

"Yes… she went to school with my husband this morning. She should be at school," I answered.

"Are you sure?" he replied.

"I'm pretty sure… What's going on?"

Well, it ended up that the bio sister had sent a text message to EVERYONE: social workers, attorneys, teachers at my child's school, and biological family. In this text message, she included the photo her friend took and something like this:

"My sister has been kidnapped. She is 4 feet tall, has brown eyes and brown hair. If you find her, please contact me immediately."

Yes, yes she did.

Well, we quickly cleared up that our foster daughter was indeed not kidnapped or missing and learned how unpredictable this sister was (fifteen-years-old at the time).

Not too longer after, our county worker approached us about starting family visits between our foster child and this sister.

"Hell, no!"

"Well," she'd said, "she has the right to request visits."

Uh, did they forget that she's out-of-control and texted everyone, including bio family, that our foster daughter had been kidnapped, with a current photo, and a message full of lies? Yes, I think they must have.

So we refused the best that we could. And in our own way.

First, we suggested letter writing. That way, the girls could ease back into a relationship and we could all monitor whether this would be a healthy relationship for our foster daughter or not. The social worker agreed to give it a few months, which we later realized meant *one* letter.

They scheduled a visit.

Which our foster daughter conveniently couldn't attend because of a school meeting. Or a dentist appointment. Or whatever else just had to be on that day during that time. I think they only had two or three in-person visits before the adoption finally cleared and we didn't have to have forced visits with this sister anymore.

Sometimes our advocacy is quiet and passive-aggressive.

Sometimes it's loud and direct. Like when the teacher tells you that your child's behavior is "typical of all male teens." I feel bad for people who make this comment because they innocently reveal their ignorance about raising a child of trauma.

So now, I look them lovingly but firmly in the eye, and I say, "I'm not angry or offended, but as the parent of a child of trauma, I need you to hear this. When you make a statement like that to someone who is raising a child with unique needs, it's very dismissive of everything we experience, day in and day out. Yes, some things will appear typical to you, and there will be overlap between 'typical' and 'unique,' but we're asking you to trust us, his parents, on this one. He will need extra help because there are things that are not typical."

Then I offer to email a few articles that I have found extremely helpful in understanding and parenting my child.

To me, the comment is like nails on a chalkboard. If you're reading this book, I'm guessing you've been to the bottomless pit of your soul with this child and are just trying to find the light, and comments like these just push you down further. Because really what the comment says is, "You're taking this way too seriously" or "What your going through is like that of every other parent who has birthed and raised their child from scratch, so suck it up."

But the school is just one of the places where we advocate, isn't it?

In California, our kids are given medical care through MediCal. However, finding doctors who accept MediCal and then getting quality care from the doctors who do accept it is a huge challenge. MediCal is just another part of the broken System we live under in California.

Doctors hate to accept it because it takes months to get paid. So the only doctors who accept it are the ones who give you five seconds of their time so they can get enough people through the door to make it worth it. We had a really hard time finding good care, though we eventually found good enough care. Nothing compared to what we could get on our own private insurance.

I tried to get on some kind of social aid in college. I didn't have a career yet that provided insurance, but I wasn't on my parents' any longer either. I walked into the office and filled out an application. The desk clerk asked, "Are you pregnant?"

"No," I answered.

"Are you failing school?"

I smiled slightly…"No."

"Then I'm sorry; we can't help you."

I'm pretty sure I just stared at her, mouth slightly ajar.

"What? You mean if I get pregnant and start to fail school, then you can give me insurance?"

Without batting an eye, "Yes, that's right."

And that, my friends, is our System.

Finding good medical care includes psychiatry. The few psychiatrists I worked with in some of the agencies I worked were just as bad. They'd come in once a month or so, see a kid for about five minutes, give an ADHD diagnosis, scribble a prescription, and rush them out the door. Parents often complained to me, their case worker, how disrespected and unheard they felt in his office. He was prescribing medication without having really heard the issue.

Not every kid needs medication! Ours don't. There isn't medicine for emotional trauma and blocks.

Now *we* might need some medication while raising them, but that's a topic in Chapter 24 under Secondary Trauma.

We have to put our foot down and be a voice. A voice that says, "NO! You will hear me and you will help me, even if it takes more than five minutes."

We have to advocate in school when our kids have serious developmental delays but nothing diagnosable to qualify for additional support. Or when teachers offer endless amounts of pity-grace because they feel bad for our kids, and then they never learn to do the work. We have to advocate when they ask for baby photos for the promotion ceremony or when they tell you that your son gets beat up at school because, well, he brings it on himself.

Our foster son was being bullied at his new school. He was punched in the stomach, slapped on the face, and verbally belittled. He was hit so hard on the head one day that his glasses flew off and broke. One of the main culprits was the daughter of a man running for district office. She stole my son's journal and wrote a bunch of profane things in his name, then turned it in to the teacher, claiming to have found it. I got a call from the principal. Now, I knew my son had some serious problems, but the language in the journal didn't sound like him. And, as we spoke, we came to realize that his name was repeatedly misspelled.

My boy knew how to spell his own name.

I met with the teacher to talk about the situation. She explained to me that many of the kids in her class came from the same nearby apartment complex and had been schooling together for quite some time. "And to be honest," she'd said, "he really brings it on himself."

Really?

This was a zero-tolerance school. Apparently it was only zero-tolerance unless you brought the bullying upon yourself.

I didn't disagree with her. My foster son wore a victim-filter. He found all sorts of ways to be the victim. It's an identity that began from a reality. He grew up in a home of extreme violence and fear. He was victimized and hadn't shaken it off.

Still. There's no excuse. He should be able to go to school and not be hit, victim or not. Immature or not. Delayed or not. Socially awkward or not.

BUT, since we didn't have educational rights, we had to subject him to that teacher and those classmates until the request to move him, with our reasons, made it through the pipeline of social workers, attorneys, and judges… and back again.

If I'd had it my way, he wouldn't have gone back to that school the next day.

We don't have educational rights unless we fight for them. Or adopt them. Whichever comes first.

Our voices got loud.

Over and over again, we find our voices needed to speak up for our kids.

We even found that we needed to advocate for our children within our faith community. We were among the first foster parents in our church and the childcare team really had no idea what to do with them. They were great to walk with us and learn, but not before some really difficult situations, like birth family members showing up and pulling the kids out of Sunday School and then "borrowing" $5 from them so they could buy "water." Five dollars they took, against court order of seeing their children, thus losing their other three young ones permanently.

Now our church has a very strict policy about who can and cannot pick up children from Sunday School. A place that is normally safe and familiar can become a danger ground when the bio family finds them and shows up.

They need our voices.

We need to teach them how to support us and our children. We are upside-down families in so many ways, families just trying to fit into the ebb and flow of every other family and social life, with all our rough edges and backwards parts. We have to help them know how to bring us into the fold.

How do we do this?

Know Your Rights

Many of us don't really know what our rights are. We simply hear the "big" folks tell us what we can and can't do, and they're not always right. You have a right to contact your child's attorney (if they have one) and get them to listen to you. If your social worker isn't sufficient for what your child needs, go to their supervisor.

Take Care of Yourself

First, this means you'll need margin in your day. Cut out the unnecessary aspects of your life right now. It's easy to resent your kid for this step, for having to cut out things you enjoy for their sake. But we have to do this anytime we have a child... it just seems to last a little longer with our children of trauma. So be it.

Our mental health matters, so carve out time in your day for rest. Because you will be making lots of phone calls, sending many emails, faxes, and letters. You will, if you're like me, be dealing daily with comments, emails, and calls from various people in your child's life. Keep one major lifeline in your life, regardless of everything else that must go. If it's time out with the ladies, do it. If it's fishing with your buddies once a month, don't stop. We need the life-giving activities in our life, and we need space. Make room for both.

Find Support

This will likely be on every list of encouragement I have for you. Surround yourself with beautiful people who get it. We asked a lovely friend of ours for any parenting advice. He and his wife have raised two biological daughters quite successfully. His response was, "How could I even begin to compare my experience of raising my girls to all of the unique needs you have raising your four? You have a very special situation and who am I to speak about that for you?" I smiled of course. And while I really did want some tips on how to raise my kids as well as he had his, his answer was spot on honest. He gets it. He gets that our situation is different. And that means so much. Whether someone has adopted or not won't always be an indicator of whether or not they can support you. His acknowledgement alone makes him a keeper, because anything else he says to us understandably comes through this filter. It validates our existence. Find those people. Let them validate your existence, remind you of your purpose, and encourage you to keep on. They might just save your life… and your child's.

Prepare for Red Tape

Okay, you can't really prepare for red tape. But you can learn to count to ten and take deep breaths. You can learn to take the new information you've been given (about everything you'll need to do just to go visit the grandparents, or to get your visa, or that they've lost your file… again) and beat your head in a pillow. My mom taught me that. Then, after the pillow beating, take your first step, and your next, one step at a time, until you make progress.

CHAPTER 7

The Challenge of Red Tape

*"Optimist: Someone who figures that taking
a step backward after taking a step forward
is not a disaster, it's a cha-cha."*

— Robert Brault, writer and journalist

A h yes, the red-tape cha-cha. If it's dancing we're doing, then our partner in the System crushes our toes, is way too short, has body odor that makes our eyes water, and leads us to dance the cha-cha while rap blares through the speakers.

Fun, right?

All of the red tape in the System, whether it's foster, private local adoption, or international adoption, is crazy. With international adoptions, you can end up with twice the tape. Someone once said that in the foster and adoption systems, there's enough red tape to wrap the globe over.

I believe it.

As if the process of filing all of the paper work, the family album, the background checks, raising the funds, finding an agency, dealing with your nation's rules, your child's nation's rules, and the agency rules weren't enough for an adoption... you get to come back to America (if you're American) and often readopt your own child on U.S. soil to get a birth certificate. When an American is born abroad, they don't have to be re-birthed on American soil to get their birth certificate.

Just saying.

The red tape is incredible. It's a huge detriment to the children and to the families wishing to foster or adopt them. More often than not, when I ask someone why they haven't chosen to foster or adopt, they can replay a few horror stories of people they know who've muddled their way, sometimes successfully, and sometimes not, through the mess of red tape.

Good families aren't fostering or adopting because of it.

Children are remaining in traumatic situations because of it.

This is absurd. It's the height of all that's wrong with our System. Fine, social workers get burned out and quit. Okay, they're not that respectful to us. Yes, we have to advocate. But this? This is possibly killing children.

It takes an average of $28,000 and 896 days to finalize a foreign adoption. Our two fost-adoptions took eighteen months and twelve months. The cost was way less than $28,000, which is good or we couldn't have done it. However, the alternative cost was the headache of living with a child that we actually had little to no rights over. We couldn't make educational decisions, medical decisions... our kids couldn't have a sleep over without permission from three different people. Seriously!

There are pros and cons to the variety of ways one can adopt a child, but all of those ways include ridiculous amounts of red tape.

We couldn't make medical decisions without all the phone calls and paperwork and conversation and attorneys and judges and workers, all over again. My friend couldn't give her foster daughter a vitamin without permission. We couldn't approve my foster daughter for an outpatient surgery removing a polyp from her lip without everyone's approval.

Somehow, we thought that after cutting through all of the red tape to even become foster or adoptive parents... that somehow they'd now trust us to do the job for which they'd approved us. I mean surely, if we could manage all of the paperwork, the signatures, the fingerprints, the baby locks, the fridge temperature, the pool gate, the background checks, the interviews of friends and family, the compiling and mailing of all necessary documents... maybe, just maybe, we'd be good enough to raise kids.

Why else wouldn't they trust us to decide if the sleepover was a good idea or not? Did they really think we were going to skip the country by going to visit my parents forty-five minutes away? Or what if we did want to leave the country? Is it so bad to show these kids the world?

We fought long and hard for a passport for our foster son. We had an opportunity to visit my husband's family on the Caribbean island where his family is from. After many hours on the phone (some of them in the passport office with the powers-that-be in Sacramento), we finally got it.

One friend said she'd been trying for five years to get a

passport for her foster child and was never successful.

It was on that trip that our foster son decided he wanted to be our forever-son. He stopped calling us by our first names and began to try out "Mom" and "Dad." He met our family and wanted to be part of it. Thank God we got through the red tape of getting a passport for our child because I think it ended up being a defining trip for our family.

But that's a big one. What about the size of the room foster or adoptive kids can live in. Or how many kids can share it. Our foster kids were required to have a desk in their room, even if they never sat at it. None of my birth children had desks, but my foster kids did! Or how about the fifty dollars per month we had to spend on brand new clothing. We couldn't count hand-me-downs or thrift stores (where we did much of our own personal shopping).

One month after one of our regular shopping trips for new clothes for my foster son, he told me that he didn't have any clothes. I asked about all the new clothes we'd just bought. He said he didn't know where they were. I went through his drawers and sure enough... gone. "Don't worry," he said, "I'll just get new ones next month."

Wow.

I still don't know where those clothes went. Probably some elementary school black market. But I do know that the System was teaching my son that his stuff was not valuable and that he didn't need to take care of it.

Because he'd just get more next month. We all know that's not real life.

We also know that getting a $20/month allowance when you're eight-years-old, regardless of whether you've run away for twenty-nine of the thirty days that month, or not lifted your finger to do a single chore, or yelled and slammed doors and broken windows, is completely unrealistic in the real world.

But that's not what the system teaches our kids. My kids learned, long before they got to me, that because they'd had rough childhoods, they deserved everything good in life without them making any effort. They were victims and they deserved a life of compensation.

And maybe they do. But life won't give them that. No one is going to keep sending them money every day of their life just for existing. No one is going to buy them brand new clothes every month just because they've been adopted. (In fact, that one stopped the day adoption finalized. They are perfectly stylish and clothed, regardless). They learned that nothing has value; it can and should be replaced. Not by them, mind you, but by everyone else.

They feel entitled. But the entitlements and the red tape are killing our kids.

In some ways, it actually physically harms them AND us.

I was a support counselor for an Intensive Treatment Foster Care program. I worked with a single foster mother and a six-year-old with Reactive Attachment Disorder (RAD). She was removed within a couple of months from every foster home because of her behavior. But each move just exacerbated her RAD symptoms and made the honeymoon in the new home shorter, and her tantrums grander.

It wasn't too long after her move into this new home that she began attacking the foster mother and me. I mean physically ATTACKING with fingernails, teeth, fists, feet, whatever she could use. The first time she launched at me was when we were working on a time-in system for disciplining behavior. She wouldn't have it. The thing about children with RAD specifically is that all parenting is upside-down parenting, much like raising any child who's been through trauma, but even more difficult. Kids with RAD need to experience that they are safe. They need to experience that you are capable of keeping them safe. Until then, they just think you're one more dangerous person.

This little six-year-old had a team of about twenty people. And you know the best they could come up with for keeping her or us safe in the middle of her physically explosive tantrums?

Lock ourselves in a room.

Because it's against the law to lock her in her bedroom. Or to physically prevent her from attacking us. One time, she took a wooden shoe shelf and threw it at us. We closed the door in time for it to shatter... yes, shatter in splinters, against the back of the door. With a piece of the splintered wood, she began to try to break her bedroom window.

And legally, we couldn't touch her. We could use our words, but she ignored those.

Again, all her team had to suggest was to lock *ourselves* away until her tantrum died down.

Let her destroy this poor foster woman's home.

Let her try to break glass with shards of wood.

Let her lunge at us with bared teeth and nails.

Because there was too much red tape to actually help her.

I understand that these rules are in place for a reason. Somebody somewhere went through all of the rigors of becoming a foster or adoptive parent and then locked their child in a closet. Or lost control of their temper and acted out physically against the child. I get it; I do.

But in order to attempt protecting those few kids (who get locked in closets and abused anyway because those same parents don't worry about the law), the System is doing more damage than good.

Actually, some of our highly traumatized children can't be helped until they're no longer under the control of the System.

Because of red tape, potential families won't even think about adopting or fostering.

Because of red tape, my extra bedroom is six square meters too small for that little girl or boy, forcing them to stay in the orphanage, in the cycle of foster care, in the traumatized situation they're in.

So why do we do this? We heard the stories, too, right? We knew how much bureaucracy there would be, didn't we? At least a little? Friends, it might be because we're a little crazy.

But if we had known ALL that we'd go through, would we still have done it? For some of us, that's a resounding "YES!" For others, it's a reluctant "Yes." Or it's a quiet "No." Maybe it's a loud "NO WAY!"

Regardless, here we are. We've done it. We're doing it. We're rising up where others have refused to go. We're treading water. We've got our big ol' gigantic scissors (or machetes, your choice) and we're hacking away at all of the barriers that stand between our children and healthy, whole lives.

Are you in the thick of this right now? Don't give up! It's hard. It's painful. It will make you want to pull the hair out of your head. Or face dive into your bed and scream. Do it. Just do it. Well, maybe not the hair-pulling.

Expect Setbacks

Seriously. You can have it all figured out, but when they lose your dossier, or the visas get delayed another month and your flight is in two weeks, or you ask your social worker an innocent question and they threaten to remove your foster child... you can sit back and say, "Ah, yes. The setback I was expecting." Okay, that's likely not what you'll do in the moment. This is usually when I bang my head onto the table and contemplate whether to laugh hysterically or curl up into a ball of tears and hibernate until the whole thing passes. And it does pass. You'll overcome this hurdle. It may not always go the way you think it will, but mountains do still move. Expect setbacks.

Start Talking

This red tape issue isn't going away. We need to start talking. We need informed, experienced people to sit down and discuss all this red tape and bureaucracy and how to eliminate as much as possible. Seriously. Kids are dying, either physically or emotionally, every day that our file sits on that desk. There has to be a better way of balancing the need for protecting our kids with laws, and actually protecting our kids.

I believe it's possible to get through the red-tape barriers. Together, we can do this. We can be a voice of reason and genuine feedback. Though I refer to the "System" as problematic (and it is) there are still many good people within it who want to help, who want to join our team of bush-whackers and get to work. Let's get savvy and work the System.

And while we're at it, let's work together about reducing the misinformation that's out there. While the System does its fair share of misleading people or offering information full of gaping holes, so does the Internet where everyone has a say. In our own arena, we can be voices of truth. At the very least, we can contribute our story to the pot. New foster and adopt parents need to know what's ahead of them and already begin setting up support systems. FFAs and counties need to know that we're letting the cat out of the bag, and hold them accountable to the misinformation that's given, both intentionally and unintentionally.

The next chapter discusses exactly this, the misinformation that's given and how we can support each other through the shock, the grief, and the surprises that often come along with it. This is a biggie. Everyone I know personally who has adopted or fostered has dealt with wrong information. How do we parent under a System that lies and/or continues to pass children around without good records?

CHAPTER 8

The Challenge of Misinformation

"Mis-information is rampant in this great age of mass-information. While we have more access to learning than ever before in the history of the world, we're actually getting dumber it seems. The amount of (mis)information at everyone's fingertips has lured us into a false sense of knowing."

—David D Flowers, writer, teacher, pastor

O ne of the great travesties of the System is all of the misinformation that is given and received. This was hard enough pre-Internet, but now with anyone posting anything and claiming it as fact, finding truth is even more difficult.

We live in a new day far removed from the one most of our parents grew up in. It has opened many wonderful doors of opportunity, but that opportunity allows for many voices to compete over each and every thought. How do we know who is right? Does the professional look of their blog give credibility? The letters after their name? Their experience? Or is it enough that they figured out how to write an article and post it? Even videos and articles that go viral may have little to do with accuracy and more to do with popularity.

And this is the climate of our hunt for help in raising foster and adopted children.

Not only is there so much misinformation out there, but now we are dealing with increased odds of being found by biological family (if that's not what we wanted). In our case, we hoped to ease our kids into a relationship with their bio families one day. But as we keep an eye on each respective family, we realize they're not ready for our kids. They're still stuck in some devastating habits. But now my kids are teenagers and interested, and here's the Internet to give them every opportunity to go around the safety of our "umbrella" or, rather, for their families to sneak around it!

Many of us tried to be good and do research on what adoption and foster care looks like. It's hard to sift through all of the info. But likely, this is where we found our agency, saw that first picture of our child, or read articles from other parents. These are so beneficial. But it's also where we read the horror stories, the miraculous nothing-has-ever-gone-wrong stories, and a few in between. We're left running the other way or filled with unrealistic hope and expectations for the experience and process.

And now we're in it.

It would be bad enough if we could blame all of our disillusionment on the misinformation of the Internet, but unfortunately, the System hands out enough of its own. Much of the time, the misinformation (or lack of information) has more to do with poor organization, an overloaded system, and the high amounts of transition.

Our file gets lost in the stack. The wrong social worker grabs our fax with theirs and trashes it. The new social worker had no idea how urgent your situation is and leaves you in the bottom of the pile. The pile that's literally six boxes high. Or, you're on the plane when the country you're headed to decides to ban all Americans from adopting their children. They told you it would take eight months, but, with all the delays and hiccups and speed bumps, it took three years. Now you have a four-year-old instead of a one-year-old. And you've missed all that life.

For those of us who've adopted internationally, you've seen pictures, spoken with the agency, and understand that kids coming from foreign foster homes or orphanages have their own unique challenges.

You go to meet your child and what you see is not what you were told, as happened to my friends, Beth and Bernard: *"Our oldest son was adopted from Madagascar at age nine and a half. After spending seven years in an orphanage eating rice, he was the size of our firstborn who was two and a half, plus we discovered he had perforated eardrums and was mildly mentally handicapped. Eventually, he was declared officially handicapped so he could be placed in an adapted educational structure (many stories of God providing there), and was able to get eardrum transplants, recuperating most of his hearing."*

Sometimes, these stories come from lack of care for each individual child, like, no one knew the child had these conditions because they just weren't cared for properly. Sometimes, I believe, these issues are hidden on purpose.

Beth went on to say, *"We've seen that so-called Christian orphanages in these developing countries (or dare I say "underdeveloped"!) often have their own cultural norms and understanding of things. Neither was ever totally honest with us; we sent vitamins, etc. to Madagascar that went to the director's kids, and our daughter never saw the photo album of family that we sent to Haiti."* Why not? Why do the things you send end up in the director's house? Why don't they see that album you slaved over?

Then there were the plain outright scummy agencies or orphanages. This devastating story comes from my good friend. And she's right, we need to talk more about these so that everyone behind us has a good shot and accurate info.

"I have found that these are the stories that aren't talked about much. They happen more frequently than I thought. In a nutshell, we were with a poorly run small agency run by a lawyer. We lived in Africa at the time. The director had no idea what was happening on the ground in DRC. She was basically just getting babies and toddlers from horrible orphanages and placing them with families. She lied to us repeatedly.

We accepted a referral for a three-year-old girl. When we got there, she was immediately taken to the clinic and was semi catatonic. We tried to get her as much medical attention as we could. She spent the entire weekend with us screaming, she had a head fungus, jiggers, scars all over her face and body, malaria, worms, open wounds on her face, her belly was distended from malnutrition, and she couldn't keep any food down.

Honestly, it was incredibly traumatizing, which sounds so selfish for me to say. The Congolese lawyer that worked for our adoption agency kept saying that it was good that we "knew Africa" so we could understand the circumstances... We had just gotten the call that my husband's mom had passed away while we were in Kinshasa and he had to fly to the U.S., and we were hit with the overwhelming responsibility of taking care of this very, very sick child and a dorm full of twenty-two boys. Our oldest son had just been diagnosed with clinical depression and we were all very weary and barely hanging on.

It seemed impossible. I would have loved to feel like I was the person that could do it, but I knew that I couldn't. Fortunately, God gave me some incredibly supportive friends who prayed and cried with me. They helped me accept our decision and they helped me grieve. One of the hardest parts in the end was that the adoption agency director was incredibly verbally abusive and kept our twenty thousand dollars. I learned a great deal about how to ask God to help me forgive and truly lay my burdens at His feet."

Maybe this isn't your story. But my friend is not alone. Or maybe it is, and now you're trying to raise this child. Or you're dealing with the grief of choosing not to be suckered into adopting a child that wasn't yours.

You're not alone. You're not crazy. And if you walked away from a bad situation, don't blame yourself.

If you've fostered kids, you know it's not much different. Getting good information on the kids seems like a valid request. Right? We specifically asked for children to be placed with us who did not have a history of sexual abuse. Knowing the long road of recovery (and the prey-to-predator statistics), we wanted to do what we could to love social orphans while keeping the kids in our home as safe as possible.

Well, a child was placed with us who, at the time, had nothing on paper about sexual abuse. But after a few weeks with him it was painfully clear that he'd experienced far more than many adults. It came out in his doodles in his third grade class, in his play with our other children, and in his conversations with new friends. He had very little memory of the actual events, but had language for things he didn't understand.

And to me, the latent, hidden, submerged sexual trauma is worse than the remembered trauma. At least from there, you can talk and work through it. In our minds, this child was a ticking time bomb. We've had a number of situations where this child crossed major lines and required more intensive therapy, not because he remembers his trauma but because he DOESN'T, even though it's there. This was the child they told us had no sexual abuse.

With some foster children, you get no medical or family history, no information on their mother's pregnancy. So you find out the hard way that they were born drug addicted or have Fetal Alcohol Syndrome. And you get to guess at their allergies and their predispositions. I was so glad when the adoptions finalized and we got their full files. SO MUCH GOOD INFORMATION! Why couldn't we have looked at that first?

All of this misinformation and lack of information is expensive. Sometimes, we pay for it financially. The adoption agency said it would only cost $10,000, but it ends up costing $30,000. Or they say there's no cost to being a foster parent, until they do the house survey and you need a ton of baby locks, a $1,500 pool fence, a new desk, a new this, a new that, a repaired this, a remodeled that. Suddenly, even foster care is expensive.

Often, the cost is emotional and physical. We are drained sifting through information, or reeling from the unexpected surprises. My friends spent $20,000 to adopt a child, not including the cost of travel and everything else, only to find they'd been lied to and scammed, empty crib and empty pockets. Yes, we cringe at the money lost. But we also relate to the heartache, the devastation, the grief and mourning that comes with the news. We take a step back, a deep breath, and try to recenter.

And all along the way, our stress levels are through the roof, on high alert for the next glitch, the next surprise, the next change in plans. And even if it never comes, the energy it takes to be looking for it, afraid of it... this is enough to keep us in bed for a long time. This is not good, healthy preparation for bringing that child home.

Wonder why parenting these kids is so hard? Well, it's hard for a million reasons.

But maybe, just maybe, one of the reasons is that we entered this thing already reeling. We weren't calm, peacefully collected, at-our-best functioning people. We were drained. We were discouraged and disappointed. Then we held that baby or child and everything behind us seemed to melt away. And praise God for that. Except that it didn't really melt away. We enter this crazy new adventure, sometimes at our lowest functioning ability. And then we just kind of hang out there... because not much is easier after that. You've been dreaming of this life, and now you have it, and it came with a few other surprises.

Because the surprises just don't end.

Spread the Word

We need to tell each other about the misinformation and wrong information out there. Be a voice where you can be. We can't change every incorrect fact on the Internet, but you have a story and it needs to be told. And I'm talking about the good ones, too. I make it a habit to share any good experience I have with a business or person because it's so easy to only share the negative. Let's direct others to good resources as well as caution them away from bad.

It Could Have Been Worse

Some of you already know that. Some of you can't imagine how it could have been. But it can always be worse. I believe that everything that happens can be used for good somehow. I don't always get to see that good or understand it personally, but still I believe it. It gives me hope that even the messiest starts can be used for the best of ends. Let's believe this together.

CHAPTER 9

❧❦❧

Recap of the Broken System

❧❦❧

"Rescuing one child from the harm of one night is glorious success. The evening is an opportunity to touch a life at a critical moment and make it better—not for a lifetime, not even for tomorrow, but for one moment. One moment—not to talk, but to act—not to change the world, but to make it better. It's all that can be done and not only is that enough—that's brilliant."

—Marc Parent, Turning Stones:
My Days and Nights with Children at Risk

What do we do with a broken system? It's clear that the many faults and failures of our government's attempt at raising children are doing a lot of harm. Fewer people are offering good homes because of the travesty of the system and all of its red tape. The homes that are taking children are exhausted, frustrated, and discouraged. Social workers are burning out and transitioning in and out all the time. How do we promote healthy families in the midst of this mess?

Do we give up? Call it quits? Discourage anyone else from adopting or fostering?

I'll be honest; I've had my moments when someone shared their "good" news of being newly certified and I cringed on the inside, knowing what was ahead for them and what that might mean for the rest of their lives. Because in those moments, I could only see the difficulties, the pain, the ongoing frustrations I still experience, even though our adoptions are finalized.

The reality is that our world is also broken. Seen the news lately? It's this top-heavy brokenness that feeds into our System. But in the midst of the brokenness is so much good.

There are families, like ours and yours, who, with machetes in hand, are tearing through the wild jungle of this life, of raising kids, of navigating through the new. We get scrapes and scratches and scars... but we just keep pushing. We could turn back. We really could. But we don't; in all our hurt and disappointment and hopelessness, each day we get up and try again.

This is enough, friends. This is amazing. At least this. We are not noble. We aren't saviors. We aren't superhuman. We're just hurting people, trying to get through the forest with our hurting kids, to make a better path for everyone behind us

This is beautiful.

There are social workers who *don't* quit. Who keep showing up, tired as they are, investing above and beyond, because they still care, because they have some power and they want to use it to help. GOD BLESS THEM! They are there. Maybe you have one.

There are agencies, like the one we had and the one I worked for, who give heart and soul to helping families navigate the

System. They become our buffer, our filter, our voice, and, often, our friends. Together, we hack our way through the jungle, but they've got a bulldozer. Sure, it sometimes gets clogged or needs a repair, but boy, sometimes these people saved our family.

And there are the children. I used to envision adoption as two paths: the one we were on, and the one our kids were on. I saw adoption like pulling the kid off of their path and bringing them to ours. A savior model. We were rescuing them from the lives they would have had if we hadn't come along and changed their journey.

I see this differently now. Instead, I see a single path of life. It has obstacles, tests, lessons, oases, deep joy. We come along and, when we adopt, we pull them to the side for just a little while. We coach them in what's to come. We give them skills, resources, and tools. We equip them for the path ahead of them. We get this time to instill in them everything we know, everything they might not have been given in their prior situations. And then, they get back on the path, still carrying their predispositions, their genetics, their birth heritage, family patterns, and their trauma. And they walk on.

And we hope and pray that we've given them everything they need.

Now we are cheerleaders, cheering them on from the side, reminding them that they are able, that their past doesn't dictate their present or their future, that they can be different. They have what they need.

They may or may not take us up on it. But whatever choices they make, what we did was right. It was good. It was better than the alternative.

We can't always see the good that comes from all of this struggle. Sometimes, it may seem like all of our heartache was for nothing.

It wasn't. It was good, though we may never know all of the reasons why.

It's changed us. We have learned real love. We've learned real pain. And I believe it's in these moments that our souls are laid bare and we become truly genuine people. We don't like what we see at first (okay, I don't like the "me" I see in some of these soul-baring moments) but slowly, the ugly is stripped away, and though we are left raw... we are left real.

Our world needs more real people.

It needs real people who are willing to be a voice, a loud one, people who will start the conversations that have sat silent, and people who will fight for justice, families, and our future: the children.

We need real people who will be peacemakers while changing the world, people who will help the rest of the world reconcile our love and our hurt, and people who will work tirelessly for the good, the muscular among us who've been hacking away at the vines for longer and endured further. We need them.

We need you.

This world needs to see love in action. It needs to see the real people, imperfect as we are, standing up every day and going at it again, loving the hard-to-love. I mean really loving them. This is not the fluff, but the stuff of every day life, the love that says "no" when it's best, the love that lets go when it's time, the love that keeps pouring into cracked jars, the love that shows up, tearstained, disheveled maybe, but present.

The System is broken.

But we don't have to be.

CHAPTER 10

The Challenge
of the Unknowns

*"I am going into an unknown future, but I'm still all
here, and still while there's life, there's hope."*

—John Lennon, singer, song writer,
and co-founder of The Beatles

W hen we adopt, we are taking in a child forever. Yet we often do this with little to no family or personal history, or inaccurate information (which we don't find out until much later). Whether we realized it or not at the time, we took in a child whose past and future are like black holes. We can't guess at what's to come, in many ways, without an accurate picture of where they've come from. This leads to living life in the wild space of Unknown. Of "surprise!"

Especially when we thought it was known.

Like the story I shared of how we requested to only take children who did not have a history of sexual abuse, and ended up with a child whose story of sexual abuses would break the box office in theaters.

We thought we were staying informed, but some information just doesn't come out for a long time.

We may have no idea that they have Fetal Alcohol Syndrome or that their hyperactivity and explosiveness is because they were drug-addicted babies. We have no idea how the pregnancy went, what mom ate or drank or smoked, and how that will affect our child. We sit in the doctor's office and they ask about the child's family history of high blood pressure, cancer rates, or allergies. And we sit dumb. We have no idea. I still have no idea.

We get kids, older kids, who have no social skills, and we have no idea what they'll need to learn until we're in a restaurant and they're leaping off the table. Or until they punch someone because they're nervous. Or until they're in the classroom and act like they're the exception to all of the rules. We look at this older child, but we can't expect all of the typical older-child social skills from them.

Surprise! When we said we'd take eight-year-olds, we expected them to act eight, not just look eight. At least in our case, their unknown experiences often delayed them in some developmental and maturity areas, which, eight years later, we are still working on.

We get kids who, on paper, are the picture of health. But we soon realize that the picture is incomplete. We took in a baby who had club feet and an internal cleft palette. Within a few months, we realized she had some vision impairment. Then she began having seizures. Then she was diagnosed with a processing disorder. And a movement disorder. And the list grew and grew.

Surprise! Your picture-of-health child has a host of conditions!

And some of these conditions will exhibit behaviorally. They will come with ADD/ADHD, destructive patterns, sexual advances, inappropriate language, survival skills that show as non-emotion or overreacting emotion. They might wet the bed clear into their preteen years. They might throw up every time you say, "No." They might throw themselves on the ground and flop and flail and scream and swear in Target, or they might attack you.

Surprise! This innocent child you've taken in acts crazy! And you endure the embarrassment, the judging eyes of others, sometimes even their comments. And you had no idea and still have no idea maybe of what to expect next.

We get kids from different ethnic groups, cultural settings, and mother tongues. We have no idea how they'll identify later. Will they reject their birth culture? Or embrace it at the exclusion of ours? Will they integrate the two? We do our best and give them the options.

Surprise! You've been raising your child to be culturally aware of where they came from, and they tell you they hate it. To never mention that place again. To never acknowledge this piece of their identity again. You have no idea if this will change or what to do.

So, we don't know the unknown, but what do we know?

We know that we chose to take these kids in. We know we already love them, even if it's just the idea of them at the moment. We know that we have a better alternative in our homes and hearts to what they've been living through. We know that our job is just to keep pouring, even if everything we pour in seeps out the cracks. We know that come what may, we have chosen this child and they are ours, even if they are also their birth family's. We know it will be hard. And we know it will be good. We may not know everything in between, but this much we do know... we said "yes," not because of their gratitude, their attitude, their grades in school, their medical history, but because we knew it was right. And they were ours.

Maybe some of those unknowns, had they been known, would have changed our minds.

Thank God, then, that we didn't know. Because these kids needed us, even if they never realized it. And maybe we need them, too.

In the next few chapters, we will work through some of these unknowns in more depth: The lack of social skills, the lack of medical history, the ways they'll respond to their world emotionally, and the ways they'll exhibit trauma behaviorally.

If you've stepped into this thing and find yourself continually surprised every day... you are not alone.

I won't be able to shine a light on everything you'll experience personally, but I can talk about common surprises that come along and help you prepare for them or assure you that your story is normal. If you need to hear that your circumstance, in light of all that seems backwards about it, is normal, then join me in the next chapter.

CHAPTER 11

❧

The Challenge
of Lack of Social Skills

❧

*"In the game of life, we all receive a set of
variables and limitations in the field of play.
We can either focus on the lack thereof or
empower ourselves to create better realities
with the pieces we play the game with."*

— T.F. Hodge, From Within I Rise

One of the great challenges of taking on foster or
adopted children is the surprising lack of social skills.
"Social skills are those communication, problem-
solving, decision making, self-management, and peer relations
abilities that allow one to initiate and maintain positive
social relationships with others. Deficits or excesses in social
behavior interfere with learning, teaching, and the classroom's
orchestration and climate. Social competence is linked to peer
acceptance, teacher acceptance, inclusion success, and post
school success."[1]

It's often a shock to find how far behind they are, or how
little they know of age-appropriate social engagement. It's
one of the unknowns that surprises you and continues to
surprise you over the course of their lives.

Why?

Social skills are acquired through observation, teaching, and practicing. All of these require consistency and continuity. Our children watch us and others. They watch how society interacts one with another, and subconsciously, they piece together what it means to be human within their context and culture. Our adopted and foster kids, however, often lack the continuity of life to observe these important skills. In the coming and going of a foster child's life, the learning of social behavior is disrupted. They are often socially awkward because they haven't had a chance to develop these skills by maintaining friendships for any length of time

Social skills are also taught. Whether we realize it or not, a healthy parent is often modeling and coaching kids on how to behave in social situations. Sometimes, this is intentional and sometimes it's an on-the-fly parenting moment where we naturally correct a child as they navigate new social situations.

Many of our foster and adopted children did not have this teaching in their early lives. How many of our kids were never put to bed? They just crashed wherever they happened to be at whatever hour sleep overcame them. Or how many of our kids never left their homes, to even have an opportunity to attempt social interactions?

And how could they have practiced what they hadn't seen or been taught?

This leads to poor manners at home and in public. They struggle with unstructured activities. They have poor work-study habits. They can't sit at a table correctly. They might make inappropriate comments or dress inappropriately. They often lack many of the executive functions, like goal setting, problem solving, and organization.

When one of our foster children was eight-years-old, we took him to a friend's house. This family had three sons and had offered to befriend our foster son. What a gift this was! Until our foster son, while two of the boys were play-wrestling, shouted out at them to "French kiss! French kiss! French kiss!" The confused boys abruptly stopped wrestling and asked their mom what "French kissing" was. Whoops.

I was so embarrassed. When we later asked our foster son in private if he knew what French kissing was, he said, "No." It was language he'd heard at home but didn't really have a definition for. (Likewise, he also had many other memories and mental images, sadly, that he had no language for). And this was minor for all that he had in store for us!

Younger children in typical families tend to learn these things through natural instruction and observation of their community. But our foster/adopt kids haven't had that chance. So they often have social skills that you would expect from much younger children. This makes relating to peers challenging. They need friends to practice... but can't seem to get or keep any among their peers. We've often been told how our oldest is so good with children. And he is! But the difference between him and some of his typical peers is that when he's with children, he becomes one. A teenage child. He doesn't maintain the role of authority or maturity. He's a great big brother but an awful babysitter.

We've also noticed when some of our younger children have passed him in certain social skills and cognitive milestones, only to see him stagger along a week or two later.

I entered a new season of life where my younger children were able to function more independently of me. My youngest had just started first grade. I was beginning to relish this new season of life... until I realized that I still had a child who required the same emotional level of attention as my toddlers once did. It was a painful and eye-opening revelation to realize that, as a mother to healthy children, I should be transitioning to this new season.

My sixteen-year-old still required parts of my parenting that I was ready to leave behind. He wasn't ready, or at the very least, he wasn't capable of stepping into the new season just yet. Sometimes I battled resentment about the ways that his delays delayed all of us as well. But I remember the hope that others have passed down, that these things will pass and one day, he can be a healthy functioning person.

They can still learn social skills.

There is so much encouraging scientific evidence about the impact of trauma on the developing brain and the hope for healing that follows. The bad news is that it's very clear that trauma in the early years of a child rewires the brain, taking development in a new direction. A direction that is challenging for them and us. Basically, when a child experiences abuse or neglect, the brain naturally triggers the fight, flight, or freeze part of the brain.

Two important things happen here. One is that over time, children can become addicted to the adrenaline of the fight, flight, or freeze rush. When this happens, they subconsciously do what they can to get you to trigger that adrenaline rush. Every time we yell or lose control of our own emotions in front of them, we push that button and they get a fix. And like any drug addiction, these kids need to be weaned off (or cut off) from this constant flow of adrenaline.

One of the hardest things about this is called a "Behavior Burst"—when we stop our part of the pattern, they increase theirs. It's sort of like they think, *Wait, this used to work before! I better try harder.* Eventually, if we form a good habit of remaining calm when they push our buttons, we can wean them off of this addiction. We have personally experienced this.

The second thing that happens is that important parts of their brain stop communicating with each other and development begins to favor the fight/flight/freeze area, which also is known for making the worst decisions (aside from survival). A traumatized child's brain tells them that every minor incident is a life-threatening occasion. Hence the public meltdowns, the explosive (and sometimes destructive) tantrums, the physical attacks on us... all because you said "no" to the candy bar. They have literally lost the ability to distinguish between a true threat and an unfavorable response.

I know, I said this was encouraging, right? Well, when I learned all of this, I was encouraged. For so long, I couldn't tell how much was intentional and how much was personality, or even, some days, if I was the crazy one. Science verifies the underlying cause of our struggle.

There's a really hilarious video on children being "brain damaged." Long before we realized our kids actually were, we would watch this video and laugh till we cried. It made us feel good to know other parents out there, any parent, sometimes looked at their kids and thought, "What in the world is wrong with you?" Okay, we don't actually SAY that to them (and if we did, we would apologize). But then we learned that there actually IS damage to the brains of these kids. It explains so much!

Perhaps some will cringe at the word "damage," and I understand why. Unless they actually get brain scans, we can't say the extent to which our kids struggle neurologically. And is it "damage" if it's just a rewiring? Whatever we decide to call it, the reality is that the trauma they've experienced has changed the anatomy of their brains in some challenging ways. This can be a lifelong change.

But it can also be rewired with treatment, sometimes medication, often specialized therapy. That's the other piece of encouragement. There's hope! Our brains have an amazing capacity to heal. Maybe we won't see that healing while they're in our homes, but we have hope (and scientific evidence) that it can happen.

These factors lend themselves to not only a lack of social skills but also many other hard-to-train skills that they need.

Your struggle is real. It's in their brains. So how do we help our kids (and ourselves) through learning new skills and rewiring their brain?

This was something I was really good at as a behavior analyst. The families I worked with were all successful in changing challenging behaviors in their homes through the methods I walked them through. I've tried many of those same methods on my own family but it's like they're immune. A method works for a week and then stops.

I can say that we worked really hard to wean our son off of his adrenaline addiction and it *worked*. We learned to respond to his button-pushing with a calm demeanor, lowered voices (when I wanted to yell, I'd lower my voice to a whisper instead), and utilizing some techniques to get his blood flowing again... like drinking a glass of water, going for a bike ride, or a moment of physical touch. ALL of these trigger blood flow and move oxygen to the brain, often getting a child unstuck from the fixated thinking. I can honestly say that our son rarely, if ever, pressures us to the point of causing enough fear in him to trigger the fight, flight, or freeze response anymore.

It stopped working. We wouldn't play the game anymore.

But there are plenty of other skills that he lacks that we have not been able to instill in him. We had eight fewer years to teach him than we have our younger two, and this has made a big difference. He is now a teenager. Lord help us all. So this is what I know and practice and encourage you in:

Patience

No matter whether we have the techniques or skills or not, rewiring a brain takes a while. It can happen. With the right help, it will happen. But it takes time. SO. MUCH. TIME. If you thought you were a patient person pre-adoption/fostering, you've probably since learned how terribly impatient you are. Welcome to the club. There's so much more growth to be had in this area.

Take deep breaths. Walk away and hide for a bit if you need to. Bite your tongue. Feel your racing heart. Learn your own triggers and the emotions you feel right before you lose it… and change the pattern. Instead of yelling, whisper. Instead of exploding, go hide in your happy place. And when you fail, extend this patience to yourself, too.

The Right Help

Brains can be rewired, but they don't usually do it on their own. It takes work. It takes the right kind of work. There are a number of programs that focus specifically on connecting disconnected points of the brain through activities and training, like Brain Spotting, a brain-based psychotherapy using the field of vision to recall traumatic and negative memories and then working to resolve them.[2] There are also many therapists who understand trust disorders, social skill training, and other issues specific to children of trauma. Find one and utilize their service. Now, if you're like us, you may not be able to afford some of the options out there. It's okay. Even if they don't get the specialize help until they're young adults, it will help.

People Who Get It (Self Care)

I'm going to sound like a broken record on this one, so I'll try to say it in a variety of creative ways. TAKE CARE OF YOURSELF! Surround yourself with others who "get it." Have a community of parents, teachers, friends who don't dismiss your experience as "typical" or suggest that you should never have adopted or fostered if it's this hard for you. Surround yourself with people who know how hard it is or believe you when you tell them how hard it is. We have some very loving, caring people who've never adopted or fostered who just take our word for it. And I love them for it. Get those kinds of people in your life and love them.

We don't realize how important our unwritten social skills are until we are in public with a child who doesn't have any. Okay, until we're in the same room with a child who doesn't have any. I remember how we'd have car booster seats at our dinner table to teach kids how to sit during a meal or how we'd role play meeting a new person with eye contact and a smile. It takes a lot of time, patience, and head-banging.

Lack of social skills is not the only unknown we deal with.

We also deal with the unknowns of their medical history, their family history, and often even their current medical situation. I have had a few moments of being dumbfounded in doctor's offices when they ask me a question I have no answer to and no way to get one. This is a reminder that even though they're mine, I didn't birth them. I don't know how the pregnancy went or whether they were born early or late or whether the biological mom had diabetes. This and more keep us reminded of what we don't know... and how important it is to know it. Join me in the next chapter to talk about this challenge of unknown medical issues.

---

1. Thomas McIntyre "Teaching Social Skills to Kids Who Don't Yet Have Them," June 23, 2006, Accessed on October, 9, 2015, www.ldonline.org/article/14545
2. David Grand, 2015, www.brainspotting. pro/page/what-brainspotting

CHAPTER 12

❦

The Challenge
of Unknown Medical Issues

❦

"Adoption is not a breaking of trust but a keeping of faith... not the abandonment of a baby but the abandonment of self for a baby's sake."

—Curtis Young, The Missing Piece:
Adoption Counseling in Pregnancy Resource Centers

T he surprises we are met with medically are exhausting. It's one thing to navigate the certification process, or deal with the brokenness of the System, but the medical surprises that come with the children are difficult to deal with. (Then again, I have at least one friend who says dealing with her son's surprise medical issues were nothing compared to the advocacy he needed to get his needs cared for appropriately!)

I find that these medical issues, specifically, are nagging reminders that I didn't birth my adopted children. When I'm asked questions that are easy to recall with my biological kids, the distinction slaps me in the face. Biological children also sometimes surprise us with their medical needs, but even in those situations, we can reflect on our own personal medical history and its contributions, or the health of the pregnancy, the condition of the birth, etc. With our adopted kids, it's just a big black hole.

The medical surprises come for a variety of reasons. In one of our situations, the child came with a few known medical needs, but as she grew and developed, more medical issues rose to the surface. Issues that needed time and the volcanic-mixture of needs her little body already had. This was no one's fault, really... it was just the nature of this poor little girl and the time it took for her needs to manifest.

For others, the medical surprises are at the hand of the agency or the orphanage. One friend recently told a story of a family who adopted internationally. When they arrived to pick up their child, the national doctor told them that their child had many medical needs, and he began to list a host of problems. The family still chose to adopt the child, and it ended up, the child had none of those needs. Was he trying to prevent the adoption? Did he really think the child had those needs? We will never know.

Then there's Laura and James's tragic story I related in Chapter 8. They still carry the emotional scars of this experience. (Not to mention the lawyer kept their $20,000). Sadly, their story is also some of yours. But some stories have happy endings like Beth and Bernard getting eardrum transplants for their deaf son.

There are story after story of children coming home with more medical needs than were ever acknowledged by the agency or orphanage. Some are so desperate to find homes for the kids that they lie. Or perhaps the orphanages are so ill-staffed that no one really knows any of the children well enough to see their needs. Orphans spending their lives untouched in a crib are all too common. It's possible that no one has ever taken the time to address their medical needs (or even acknowledge them) until we come along.

I heard a story on the radio one day. A Christian musician shared that his wife wanted to adopt children who were terminal, in order to give them the best possible last few days, weeks, or months of their lives. I wept at their story. In their situation, they were going in knowing that these kids were bottom-of-the-list, least-likely-to-survive, children. When the rest of us take these kids, we expect them to live. Still, it's more evidence to the fact that many children are suffering and dying in orphanages every day. We hope to help, but our help is limited. It takes all of us, with our different callings and capacities, to meet this need.

Whether you go into adoption or foster care expecting the medical needs or not, they are hard. They require long-suffering. We are often told that our child is healthy or has minimal needs, only to find that the needs are quite grave and the ability to meet them is daunting. As my friend said, the medical needs of her son were manageable, but getting the care they needed to help him was nearly their undoing.

If this is you right now, and you are spent to the bone, you are not alone. I know that doesn't lighten the actual load you are facing. It doesn't touch the sleepless nights or the endless screaming of your child, or the g-tube feedings, or the seizures, or the treatments needed. But I hope you hear that we get it. There are others who understand. It's okay to cry, to yell, to question, to regret, to cry some more.

It is.

Because this is part of your journey. This is your story. And there is good in it yet. Friend, if I could take your hand and squeeze it... I wouldn't have a lot of words, but I'd smile, hug you if I could, and say, "I know... I know."

My friend Janet is raising the most medically complex child I've ever known. We had this child for a handful of her first years before she was moved to a medically fragile home. We've stayed in touch and now, from the sidelines, I've watched in wonder, in awe, and sometimes despair, at the amount of effort required to care for this child. Her story could be another book. I have, however, asked her what she'd share with others in similar circumstances.

She said, "*Expect the unexpected. Find good doctors who listen to you and whom you trust. Find a few strong friends that you can turn to for support. Allow others into your world and don't shut people out. I often 'trade' children with them for the day, which gives us a break and a better perspective that then allows us to provide greater support for each other.*

I personally look for the positive in each new and/or declining condition. I thought that the ventilator support at night was going to be awful but the positive is it allowed me to spend extra quality time with her. Watching her peacefully sleep is a blessing, as I'm able to chat with a friend [that's me] across the world at 3 am. Focus on the small details and don't become overwhelmed by the large painting. Enjoy every minute. Don't let frustration consume you, as it steals your joy."

She says all of this, knowing that in one month, her eight-year-old daughter will have surgery for new ear tubes, a lung wash, and a trach revision. Naturally, we are praying for no complications, as we've prayed for the last eight years for this sweet child.

Get Sleep

I know this sounds silly, or perhaps even impossible. But caring for a child with special needs is physically and emotionally exhausting. I know from experience! If you're both home, tag-team the care with a spouse or partner so one of you can rest. If you need a babysitter so you can take a nap or have a respite for a few hours… hire one! You can hire someone to clean your house, but only you can be mother or father to your child, and the only way you can be the best at that is to be rested. Truly. No matter how much love, how much skill, how much equipment, if you're sleep-deprived, you won't be any good to anyone. Make good sleep a priority.

For some of our children, the needs are not so much medical as emotional. While we have cared for a child with severe physical needs, our experience lies more in raising children with emotional delays and blocks. Friends, this has probably been the hardest part of my personal journey, and it has lead to Secondary Trauma (which I discuss in detail in chapter 24). I had no idea the toll that this would have on me or my family. If you've battled the emotional blockade of your children, then join me in the next chapter to talk about what this looks like for our children, for our homes, for our own sanity, and the hope we can find while parenting them.

CHAPTER 13

❧❦❧

The Challenge of Emotional Delays and Blocks

❧❦❧

"My friends, adoption is redemption. It's costly, exhaustive, expensive. And outrageous. Buying back lives costs so much. When God set out to redeem us, it killed Him."

—Derek Loux, Christian musician and father
of ten children (eight adopted)

A s if the medical uncertainties weren't enough, most of us will also deal with emotional and psychiatric surprises.

The more I read, the more I realize how unsurprising it is that our adopted and foster children have these needs for emotional healing.

Michael DeBellis, in his 2001 article on developmental traumatology, said that "Violence and traumatic stress are both linked to the neurobiological systems that affect physical health as well as cognitive functioning, emotion control, and behavior."[1] This explains a lot. If your child even witnessed violence or abuse, the stress-damage has taken its toll and requires a lifetime of healing.

The good news is the healing. It's possible. I haven't seen it entirely in my own children. But I keep believing. The brain is an amazing thing. The more I study it, the more I'm in awe of the creativity and detail of it. It can heal.

And boy, do we ever need it healed!

If you've fostered or adopted, you've seen what the emotional trauma of our children can look like. I don't know about you, but this is what most exhausts me at the end of the day. The emotional energy it takes to parent their emotional-deficits and damage. The metaphoric fire extinguisher I walk around with all day, putting out the many small fires of my emotionally delayed but super-charged child.

Some of the emotional surprises we've encountered are explosive anger, passive-aggressive anger, withholding emotion, attention seeking through physical and emotional pain, victim mentality, trust/attachment issues, resentment toward biological kids, maturity delays, fear and anxiety, emotional clinging, sense of time (behaving now as though there were no consequences for present actions), pleasure driven, and self-protection/guardedness.

Each of the needs in that list represent story after heart-breaking story of children who live with a victim mentality, who won't take any responsibility for their own choices, and who somehow always find the bully and become his or her target. There are stories of children with trust and attachment issues, who are charming and lovely outside of the home, but emotional energy sappers at home.

There are kids who will walk off with a stranger, all smiles and chatter, but not look you in the eye or sit near you at home. There are kids who resent your biological children because they get the happy childhood they never had. And being too immature to understand that, they begin to act out physically and verbally toward the other kids in the home. Then there are kids who look ten on the outside but can only be expected to act five or six. The list is heavy, isn't it?

I know you're nodding your head, examples coming to your own mind. I wish I could hear them, because I know I'd relate, and we'd bond over this shared experience.

Because there is something about doing this together that makes it a little lighter. And if nothing else, sharing our stories and listening to others both makes us grateful that ours isn't as bad as *theirs*, and likewise, encourages others that at least their journey isn't as rough as ours. There's always room for some gratitude, right?

Most of the anger we've experienced (from our children) has been passive-aggressive. Some of you may prefer that to the explosive kind... and perhaps, in some ways, I do too. But I've sometimes felt like the verbally abused-spouse who just wishes her husband would hit her so she could prove to herself and others that she's truly abused.

I had a child who I sometimes wished would just punch a hole in the wall. I could take a picture and show people what it's like to live with him. Because they don't get it. They saw his charm, his fun personality, his ability to serve others with a smile. They didn't get to see the silence at home, the ways he'd steal and lie, the smile to our faces while he slandered us when our backs were turned. But if he'd just punch a hole in the wall... I could show them.

We also had a child who, from very young, used pain to get attention. I imagine that in his home, sharing two parents with fourteen siblings, he didn't get much attention, except negative attention. Perhaps with pain, he'd earned his parents' focus for a minute. And that trick transferred with him from home to home until he reached ours. Being the good behavior analyst that I was, we nipped that in the bud.

We stayed unaffected by minor injuries (if there was even an injury at all) and gave him lots of positive attention for other, more appropriate interactions.

As he got older, he realized that emotional pain got him a lot of attention also. He began to share false stories of emotional pain with his teachers, his youth group leaders, or whomever would listen. He would take a sentence from us such as, "We don't need you to do your chores. We can do them for you," and tell people, "My parents said they don't love me and they don't need me."

Naturally, listeners would panic for him and smother him with the attention he was seeking, feeding it. His stories often revolved around us and ways we caused his pain. This was devastating to us. We were new to our community, so people didn't know us well yet. In our previous community, people would have already known about some of his issues and responded in a way that was truly helpful to him and us.

Fortunately, after a couple of years in that setting, people got to know all of us and could see that we are not an abusive family. We love all of our children and care for him as for any of the others. They could see that the stories he wove didn't hold up.

In this time, he also built a reputation for himself among his peers and others for being dishonest, for being a "mooch," and for manipulating. While this put his peers at arm's length away and broke our hearts to see how few good friendships he had, it also alleviated some of our stress regarding the slander he'd spread about us.

Many of you know exactly what I'm talking about. Way too many of you have had Child Protective Services called on you because a well-meaning person listened to your child in all their trauma, and rather than approaching you about it, made a phone call.

I have a dear friend who can't take an exchange student because of the few reports filed against her due to her adopted teenager's slander. ALL of the reports were unfounded... yet, they stay on her record, and she can't house an exchange student. This same friend, though a stay-at-home-mom now, is a teacher by career. She worries that because of the attention-seeking behavior of her daughter, she won't be allowed to teach children should she decide to pursue a job.

How many of us live in that terror? Do you fear CPS leaving a card on your door or showing up to interview your other children? Do you worry that this one kid could ruin your career, your family, your ability to serve others in certain capacities? How about the fear that they'll believe your child and take all of your kids away? I've known families who stopped fostering for this very reason. The kids were too "dangerous" for the family, not in their explosive violence, but in their loose, attention-seeking tongues.

Psychiatric Surprises

In 2007, The Casey Field Office Mental Health (CFOMH) completed a study on the lifetime mental health disorders of adolescents in foster care, ages fourteen to seventeen-years-old. Using the Composite International Diagnostic Interview (CIDI), they assessed the prevalence of mental health diagnoses among this population of foster children. White, Havalchak, Jackson, O'Brien, and Pecora found that "Most youth in foster care come from a traumatic family history and difficult life experiences [including removal from their birth family], increasing their risk for mental health disorders.[2]

A study in 1999 by Dubner and Motta of children in foster care revealed that Post Traumatic Stress Disorder (PTSD) was diagnosed in 60% of sexually abused children and in 42%

of the physically abused children. The study also found that 18% of foster children who had not experienced either type of abuse had PTSD, possibly because of exposure to domestic or community violence.

They found that *one in five* of these foster children have three or more lifetime diagnoses (ADHD, Depression, Post Traumatic Stress Disorder, Oppositional Defiance Disorder, Conduct Disorder, and Panic Attacks), compared to the 14.7% of the general population of children in the same category. And about three in five foster children had at least one of the lifetime diagnoses, versus the 45.9% of the general population. This was significantly higher than rates of their sample of non-fostered children.[3]

Other psychiatric issues I've seen personally are developmental delays, psychological stress and confusion, Fetal Alcohol Syndrome / Alcohol Related Neurodevelopment Disorder, Reactive Attachment Disorder, and Intermittent Explosive Disorder. They also lack many of the executive functions such as management and regulation of working memory, reasoning, task flexibility, problem solving, planning, and execution. One of my children, in particular, seems completely incapable of any form of organization, of goal-setting, of planning ahead, or reasoning through a discussion, or of remembering things we've said daily for the last eight years.

While I realize that this chapter has gone all technical on you, I share it because *there's a reason* our kids are the way they are. Of course we know this somewhere in the back of our minds. Or at the very least, we recognize that something to do with their trauma has altered the way they do life. And much of that alteration affects us and our lives as much as theirs.

As I mentioned above (and in Chapter 11), the literal and physical changes of their brains, because of early physical abuse, sexual abuse, neglect, and the witnessing of violence, alter the chemistry and physical pathways of the brain. They've been wired for survival. But staying in survival mode THAT LONG continues to do more damage to their physical health and emotional well-being.

Hence the big diagnoses in adolescent and young-adult years.

The good news is that we're not crazy. Our kids *are not typical*. I mean, typical kids are hard enough! But our kids come with all these additional "surprises" that take our breath away. Literally.

Sometimes, I've just needed my struggling child to go away for a couple days so I could breath. So I could regroup and go at it again because this is for the long-haul. We're in it. Now what?

There's hope. The fact that studies are being done and people are talking is a great first step. Awareness often leads to help. More therapists are prepared to help us into a greater sense of well-being. We've pulled from our small savings to hire an out-patient service to help provide mediation, coaching, and training in the areas that relate to our own mental health and our children's.

Though we hired the service for one particular child, they offered help to all of us. I utilized my coach by phone, to vent, to process, and to glean whatever insight they have from their years of experience working with kids who were just like mine, and I love that. It shows me what's possible.

Maybe, one day, my son will share his story with others and help other kids who are just like he once was.

Get Help

This will likely come up multiple times, especially again in Chapter 24. But really… get help for them and for yourself. I'm a counselor, so I'm biased, but I think we should ALL have someone to talk to, someone who can listen without judgment, or somewhere we can dump our own brains in a healthy space, so that we can keep on with the hard work.

Step Back

Find a way to pull yourself outside of the emotionally-charged situation. I say this, knowing FULL WELL how crazy hard this is. But man, when you can do it, the result is night-and-day different. Don't take their emotional delays personally. Don't take their lack of maturity personally. When they target their pain toward you, step back. Love them. Encourage them. But don't take on their stuff as a personal weight.

There's a FABULOUS article by Mark Hutten called "Parenting Children and Teens with Reactive Attachment Disorder." He warns that as parents of children of trauma, we should not care more about our child's problems than they do. Typically, these kids will find themselves quite content to let us do the stressing and worrying over their decision, while they continue making the poor choices. He reminds us that we cannot make our children better or successful. They need to do the work of growing. "In the spirit of counter intuitiveness, acknowledging that your youngster has the freedom and the power to make a mess of her life increases the chances that she won't."[4]

Even if your child isn't diagnosed with RAD, most foster and adopted children have some kind of trust disorder. We have found this particular strategy, of not caring more about their decisions than they do, to be supremely helpful with our kids, even though only one has a formal diagnosis. And them aside, we are healthier people when we don't take the responsibility and anxiety of our children.

Say our child is failing his classes at school. It's easy for us to worry about the possibility that he won't graduate high school, that he won't get into college, that he'll spend his life digging ditches simply because he won't turn in his homework. Instead of burdening ourselves with all of that, we might share some of the possible consequences of his action and then say, "But hey, it's your life to live. You make your decision and we will support you. If you want to succeed in school, we're here to help. If you don't, then carry on. It's you who will live that life, not us." Suddenly, we've handed him the responsibility of carrying the greatest concern for his choices.

This becomes especially important when their emotional trauma manifests in behavioral problems. I believe all behavior has a source in a belief, even if it's deep down. We and they may never know or understand that belief, but all the same, it's contributing to some out-of-control behavior. And this behavior is often embarrassing for all of us. We begin to avoid public outings, time with friends, and try to manage everything from within our house. But then they go to school or church and the issues are unavoidable.

In the next chapter, I discuss the surprises we face in behavioral challenges and ways to remain healthy, hopeful, and productive.

1. Michael D. De Bellis, Developmental Traumatology: The Psychobiological Development of Maltreated Children and Its Implications for Research, Treatment, and Policy, Developments in Psychopathology 13, no. 3, (Summer 2001): 539-64, accessed October 10, 2015, www.ncbi. nlm.nih.gov/pubmed/11523847

2. C. R. White, A. Havalchak, L. J. Jackson, K. O'Brien, and P. J. Pecora, Mental Health, Ethnicity, Sexuality, and Spirituality Among Youth in Foster Care: Findings from the Casey Field Office Mental Health Study. (Seattle, WA: Casey Family Programs, 2007). 13.

3. A. E. Dubner and R. W. Motta. "Sexually and Physically Abused Foster Care Children and Posttraumatic Stress Disorder," Journal of Consulting and Clinical Psychology 67, no. 3 (June 1999): 367-373, www.ncbi.nlm.nih.gov/pubmed/10369057

4. Mark Hutton, "Parenting Children and Teens with Reactive Attachment Disorder," accessed October 10, 2015, www.reactiveattachment-disorder.com/2009/07/ parenting-children-with-reactive.html

CHAPTER 14

The Challenge of Bad Behavior

"A wise man is superior to any insults which can be put upon him, and the best reply to unseemly behavior is patience and moderation."

—Moliere, French playwright and actor

N aturally, the many surprises we face in the emotional and psychiatric arena of our children lead to a plethora of behavioral manifestations. There are plenty of books and articles on the many ways to deal with our child's behavior.

But like every parenting book and paradigm and issue, you have to find what works best for you and your family.

Personally, we've found that most everything works for about a week, and then stops. Eight years in, we've depleted our ideas. Every one of them. Some days, we feel like we're just clinging to a sinking life raft in the middle of a tumultuous sea. No rope. No helicopter. No land. No food. Just shark fins and waves. And we keep trying to plug up the holes, but the air still comes out.

Oh, you too?

We've handled bedwetting, lying, stealing, cutting, hoarding food, overeating, shadowing, crazy sleep habits, impulsivity, narcissism, slander, physical violence against siblings, manipulation, and poor (very poor) academic performance.

We've also dealt with sexual issues, the very thing we tried to avoid. We've had pornography, cross-dressing, sexualized play, sexualized drawings, sexual comments, and inappropriate physical and emotional boundaries with the opposite sex.

Sometimes relationships are viewed as completely platonic while not maintaining clear and healthy emotional and physical boundaries. This child over-touches everyone. It's not even sexual to them, it's simply a confusion over the use of touch. I understand that in the climate of America today, some of the things on that list are not seen as problematic or even an "issue." However, given the history of this particular child, these are clearly related to early abuse.

My dear friends, Charles and Katherine, experienced this in a horrifying way. Biological relatives of their three children in guardianship withheld important information until it was too late. Their oldest child in guardianship had likely been molested, watched porn, and sexually acted out on his two younger siblings prior to placement. This wasn't revealed until he had been in their care.

He left a trail of destruction with a number of other

"girlfriends" that were not reported by the county. Following the removal of this particular child, his younger brother proceeded to molest their three-year-old biological son. In the midst of all of this, the sister, who remained in their home, was kidnapped one day on her way to school, molested, and left for dead by a stranger. Against the odds, she survived and made her way to help. She was only ten.

For Jenny, a crazy difficult aspect was not getting enough info on their child beforehand. One of their kids had been in foster care for over two years. When the girl came, she had no medical info and no history of her last placements. They were never told that she had a history of animal abuse. They should have had at least two years of medical history and at least two years of records stating why she was moved from every placement. They had no idea that she had previously abused animals in former placements until she killed their cat.

In addition to the behavioral challenges we meet with at home, many of our kids also have academic surprises.

Often our kids end up with learning disabilities, poor study skills, poor organizational skills, and trouble with peers. One of my children, when in sixth grade, had tutoring every day on his school campus. On his way to tutoring, he would throw away his homework. Upon arriving at tutoring, he'd tell the tutor that he didn't have any homework. When asked why he was throwing it away, he said, "It looked too hard." Well, it probably was, that was the point of the tutoring!

Another child had an in-home tutor. He did worse on his post-tutoring assessment than his pre-tutoring assessment! We've had kids lack all motivation for anything school-related, except the social aspects. We've had so many meetings with school counselors, school psychiatrists, teachers, guidance counselors, you name it. And you know what? He never qualified for additional services because he tested low-average on all of the assessments. He was "capable" but we believe his emotional blocks were so strong, he didn't perform, even within his ability.

On the flip-side, we had a child who was in second grade doing kindergarten work. By the end of her third grade year, she had not only caught up on the two years she was behind, but moved to the head of her class academically! We later found a note that she'd written to her biological mother. In her note, she told her mom that she should be able to come home soon because she had straight A's.

She thought she was removed from her home because of her grades. Or, at the very least, that if she did better, she would be able to go back.

We talked her through the reality of that situation (that it wasn't her school work) and still, she persisted in high academic success. Even years after the dream of going home faded, she continued to excel. Why? Well, I'm sure there are a number of reasons, but one reason I've seen (and encouraged in other kids) is that the rest of life may be out of control, but they can control their school career. So much of her life had been out of control, but she saw that she could at least control her success at school. And she has.

While many would hope that their children would deal with trauma in this way, it came with its difficulties as well. She was a perfectionist who set a very high standard for herself and others (so high that many times, she and her friends couldn't meet it). Her high achievement sometimes led to a superiority complex. Mostly, though, it gave her a sense of guardedness. She was super skilled in keeping people at an emotional distance. She controlled every aspect of what you knew about her. She was like walking armor.

I knew she was in there, but she'd walled herself in, keeping up a facade of perfection so no one could really see how broken and hurt she was. In fact, I'm not sure she let her own self see how broken and hurt she was. We caught glimpses periodically, like when she couldn't keep up the facade and felt that parts of her identity were crumbling, and she began to hurt herself, either burning eraser marks into her skin or poking her hands and arms with a safety pin.

So yes, the daily living with her was so much easier than all of the meetings and comments and hardships of her brother, but it's still just another survival skill. And it's harder to see and deal with because it's not so blatantly detrimental.

Every year, I start off hopeful that my older son will pass his classes, that he won't be expelled, that maybe, just maybe, this will be the year things click.

And for her...I hope that this year, maybe, just maybe, will be the year she lets herself be human, and lets us love her anyway.

I've read so many books and articles on the topic of managing behavior, and there is a wide spectrum of options. On one end, you have people who say that the only way to change behavior is to get to the heart of the child and issue. On the other side, you have those who say behavior can be changed by conditioning, by negative and positive reinforcements. There is much I agree with on both sides.

I agree that the heart is important. And I also agree that behavior can be changed by external measures. Sometimes, I'm too exhausted for another three-hour session with the heart (which we've done, usually late into the evening), and other times, I've used all the tools in my toolbox and have nothing left for that behavior. I'm of the mind that sometimes, the heart can't be reached when the behaviors are totally out of control.

Give Yourself Grace

Be patient with yourself as you try and find what works for your family. Sometimes, nothing will work. Embrace the empty toolbox and pray a lot. If you don't pray, this would be a good time to take it up. Make peace with your situation (for your own good). Call it what it is: difficult, frustrating, exhausting. Then give it permission to take its course while you find a happy place.

Get Outside Help

With extreme behavior, I think getting outside help is so important. I've sometimes been the help and seen what a difference my presence and skill-set make. If nothing else, locked in our own cage, we'd sing High School Musical's "We're All in This Together," and find a way to laugh about it. Together. Because we shouldn't do this alone. It's not good for us or our kids. This is a season. Find help. Even if it's just for behavior initially.

Adoption is *forever*. We step into this permanent relationship with very little information or with information that ends up being incorrect, incomplete, or skewed. We don't always realize the impact this will have on us until it hits. Those moments when you think, "This is not what I signed up for." Believe me, we've had those moments.

We've dealt with many surprises with our kids in the areas of social skills, medical conditions or needs, and emotional and behavioral manifestations of trauma. Eight years into our adoption stories, we are still often surprised. Life is full of them, isn't it? We can spend all of our time begrudging and resenting each surprise, or we can take it as a new test toward getting a master's degree in our children. We can take it as an opportunity to define who we are as we seek to love the hard-to-loves.

In the next chapter, we will discuss the challenge of parenting. Yes, it's a challenge for any parent. But we get to deal with the nuances of raising blended families, of not sharing those first moments or years of life with them (except for a handful of us), of diving into parenting older kids when we've never parented any kids, or working through our attachment and their attachment... or the lack of attachment.

Parenting is hard.

Parenting children of trauma is especially hard. The next chapter spends time on these issues and ways we can come through them strong.

CHAPTER 15

❧❦❧

The Challenge of Parenting

❧❦❧

"Your 'success' as a foster or adoptive parent is not measured by your capacity to keep everything in order; it's determined by your ability to trust that even in the chaos, Jesus is beautiful - and even in the mess, so is what you are doing for these kids."

—Jason Johnson, foster and adoptive father and writer

Parenting is the hardest thing I've ever done, hands down. Initially, I thought it was marriage, but the kids proved me wrong. Does hard mean unlovable? Does it mean wrong?

No.

While it's the hardest thing I've ever done, it's also the most rewarding and the most life-changing. Parenting is the "school" that has taught me the most about myself and has grown me into, hopefully, a wiser person. I joke that my oldest reminds me how much I need Jesus. He doesn't use words. His life says it. He brings me to my knees ALL THE TIME. And while I don't want hard things in my life to bring me to my knees... *I need them.*

That being said, there are days when I have nothing left to give. I have no more answers, no more solutions, I don't even have one more idea on how to make this easier or better. I'm spent. I'm exhausted. I want to find a rock and crawl under it so that all of the people who want to comment, email, or phone me about my kids won't be able to find me. They'll have to just figure it out, like we've been doing. I'm not kidding.

If someone gave me a dark, small place to hide, I would have been in it. I have been so low in this job at times that I can hardly function. But kids have a way of preventing parents from checking out. My youngest two, especially, still need me to be very present. To cook their meals, help them get ready for school, help them with their homework. They pull me back into the life I sometimes try to hide from. (When I escape to the bathroom, they're there. When I go to the depths of my basement, they find me, the little stalkers.)

Parenting any child is hard. It's an under-appreciated, mostly thankless job. Foster and adoptive kids will sometimes take out the anger about their lives on you. That's when they yell, "You're not my real parents," and storm out. And this, my friends, can be a good sign. Sometimes, it shows that they trust, deep down, that they can treat you this way and you'll continue to love them.

But sometimes, it's still their trauma railing against you, convinced that you'll kick them out anyway, so let's get it over with, in which case, we have an opportunity to prove them wrong.

When our adopted kids started to talk back, we cheered in private (and nipped it in the bud in public). We cheered because they'd never trusted us enough to talk back, never trusted that our lives together would go on, that we'd stay their parents and they'd stay our kids. Do I love the back-talking? No way! Except that it shows progress.

Some of us took in kids before we'd ever raised any. We went from childless-adult to parenting a baby, a toddler, an older child, a pre-teen, or a teenager. Talk about diving in with both feet! You have no idea what your parenting style is. You have no idea what "normal" is; you have to figure it all out WHILE raising these big kids.

We have to do this as parents of birthed children, too, but at least we have nine months or so to prepare for the life we anticipate. As women, we get to "know" and fall in love with the child almost a year before we're holding them in our arms. As men, you watch your woman's womb stretch and grow with the life you've created, preparing physically and emotionally for the day this child enters your lives. We and our children learn together. They're too young to realize that we have no idea what we're doing.

I love my children, all of them, regardless of who birthed them.

And I have unique bonds with them, depending on experiences we've shared. Sometimes, I look at my firstborn and I remember how hard it was in those first six weeks. There were so many books, articles, blogs, videos, friends, and strangers trying to be a voice into our situation. I took the advice and very little of it worked for us. When I finally tossed most of it out the window and did what worked for us, we found peace in our home. We ended up with a variety of tips from an array of sources, all mashed into our lives.

He cried a lot. I cried a lot. But we worked it out. We made our way through the trenches, new mama and new baby, and that is a bond I will always have with him.

Like strangers who survive a tragedy together and come out the other side forever connected. That's how I feel, like we survived and wow. Three months into that is when our first foster child came and I skipped from mothering a three-month-old to mothering an eight-year-old.

It takes time to find your parenting style. Isn't this the joke about every firstborn? Parents make the mistakes on them and have it figured out for the next child? (I'm a firstborn, so this frustrates me as much as anyone else, but now, as a mother, I totally get it). And our foster and adopted kids come to us having experienced a gamut of parenting styles. They're already wired for survival, so any sign of insecurity from us, and they'll quickly try to take over as authoritarian. They want to feel safe, and if we can't make that happen, then they'll do it themselves. I've worked in homes where the three-year-old ran it all. They don't want to be the adult, but someone has to be.

So we step into this space with children, some of us having never parented before, with the great pressure from us and them to get it right. And even for those of us who have parented, every kid is so different! Their needs are different. Their triggers are different. Their personalities are different. What works for one might not work for the rest. If this is true in a home without adopted children, how much more so with them! They bring their genetics, their predispositions, their survival skills.

And once you figure it out, they change. You finally find what motivates them, and it lasts two weeks. Or you put in a ton of hard work, blood, sweat, and tears, day after day, year after year... and then one trigger seems to unravel it all. It can take a long time to get our kids into a good space, but it can take a moment to undo it.

Then, if you're like me, you finally run out of ideas.

But I'm a behavior analyst. I don't run out of ideas. I have a HUGE toolbox of ideas. And, just to break out of the box, I've got all the books and workshops and webinars on the other side of the parenting paradigms, of how to love our children enough, pour into them enough, shepherd them enough, and still nothing.

I've tried it all and I have had nothing left.

We want to understand their emotional reactions and know how to respond in a way that brings them comfort and healing. But sometimes, we're just plumb out of ideas.

Those are some of my lowest points. I get a text message about our child. My husband says, "What should we do?" and I say, "I have no idea." We sit there quietly, searching space for a sign or an answer. We pray. We beg. We sleep on it.

Ideas come to mind but we've "been there, done that, and it didn't work." We have the heart-to-heart conversations and then the kids turn around and do it again and again. This article says I'm wasting words on a fool; just tell him what to do. The lady on the webinar says to always reason with them like adults and give them chance after chance.

To be honest, listening to it anymore is exhausting. Listening to everyone's ideas on what I should try next is enough to put me in a fatigue-coma. And I still have two or three or four others in the house who need a healthy mama. They need their hearts reached before it's too late.

The act of parenting can bring me so low.

But then I get a kiss on the cheek.

Or he pulls out his homework and works on it unprompted.

Or she comes and sits on my bed and shares her life.

Or in front of his friends, he runs and hugs me.

Or a note under my door with scribbles from her heart.

Or breakfast on the table on Mother's Day.

A Pepsi in my Christmas stocking.

These moments remind me that some good is in there. These kids and their hearts and their hopes... beautiful glimpses. And renewed motivation to press on. And courage. And hope.

This beauty and possibility is in all of our kids, no matter how far gone they seem. Maybe they don't even realize it themselves, but that time will come.

In the meantime, how do we stay healthy? How do we take care of ourselves? Our other children? Our spouses?

Respite

Every parent needs some respite. You need it, I need it. We need a weekend away, a night away, hours away. We need to check out, clock out, and have time to recover, to remember how to take deep breaths. Some of us have official resources for respite (i.e., foster parents) and some of us have to find it in our community. Be bold to ask for it. And be clear about what you'll need. Only use people you know you can rely on. You don't want someone who will flake out on you at the last minute. Maybe you respite swap with another family. But find this.

Remembering the Moments

Don't let go of the moments that remind you why you're doing this. Make a photo album of them. Write them in a journal. Share them with friends. I so easily get caught up in the HARD that I miss the GOOD. I forget the progress. I lose my "WHY." Don't let this happen! Keep a record of every right. Cling to those moments that felt like treasure, that felt like, "Oh, YEAH! This is why we do this." The old Creative Memories slogan for the making and preserving memories is to "experience the past, enrich the present, inspire hope for the future." It's brilliant. This is something I work on for all of us, through digital albums, photo cards, whatever. However I

can remind each of us how much good we've experienced, the more I fight the mind-battle that everything is bad.

CHAPTER 16

The Challenge
of Trauma Versus Typical

"To be loved but not known is comforting but superficial. To be known and not loved is our greatest fear. But to be fully known and truly loved is, well, a lot like being loved by God. It is what we need more than anything. It liberates us from pretense, humbles us out of our self-righteousness, and fortifies us for any difficulty life can throw at us."

— Timothy Keller, author of The Meaning of Marriage

Anyone who has ever spent any length of time with children can guess at what it must mean to live with them. But most often, we don't really understand until they live with us.

When our first foster child joined us, I'd been working with children for years. I spent time in their homes, with their families, observing them in school, taking them on outings, all for about an hour at a time. Then our first foster child came.

After an hour, I was like, *Sooooo, normally I'd be going home right now, but this is my home and you now live in it. What to do.* I had to get creative. And that's when the reality of parenting kicked in. This wasn't a friendly home visit. This wasn't me guiding other parents in what to do. This wasn't a fun hour-long outing to get "in" with the kid and give the parents some respite.

This was my new life.

And he wasn't going anywhere.

At least not in the foreseeable future.

Duh-duh-duh.

I offered him a snack. I began to cook dinner. I made small talk. And I internally pleaded with my husband to come home from work so we could tag-team this. I mean, I had a three-month-old baby to care for, but that was nothing compared to dropping an eight-year-old on your porch.

So I did what I knew how to do.

I gave him lots of charts, schedules, and social stories books. I leapt into all of my training as a behavior analyst.

But he didn't need a behavior analyst; he needed a mom. And that took me some time to figure out.

If you don't have biological kids, it's hard to know what is typical behavior and what is trauma-based behavior.

For the first time in our parenting experience, our biological son has reached the age of our first foster placement when he moved in.

We have now lived the eight years we missed with our oldest. SO MUCH LIFE happens in those first years. The rapport, the bond, the trust, and the depth of experience we have with that biological child is everything we lacked when our oldest showed up, a dazed, confused, and broken stranger. He was always very tense when people touched him, though he over-touched everyone else. We don't have that with our now eight-year-old biological son. It's heartbreaking. It reveals what we missed, what he missed, well, what my oldest two both missed.

We don't know, yet, if the middle school years will look the same, or the high school years, until we're walking them. And even then, our small sample size of two and two isn't a valid comparison of "typical" older adopted kids and "typical" bio kids. Because they're ALL challenging in their own special ways. There are plenty of biological children who have out-of-control behaviors. And there are plenty of adopted kids who are well-behaved.

So how do we know? And does it matter?

Well, it matters to my I-like-to-understand-everything self. I like a label so I can understand it. I like a diagnosis because it means I'm not alone. People have been down this path before because, whatever it is, it has a name. And a name means a trail-blazed pathway.

But it's not that easy with our kids, is it? I mean, we have people all the time saying that what our kids do is a "typical teenage boy thing" or a "typical teenage girl thing" to do. And sometimes, I agree... but other times, I can't believe how blind they are. Or how few teenagers they must spend time with. Because at least one of my kids seems to magnify "typical" to its extreme.

Most typical teenage boys that I personally know can be left home with their siblings without consistently causing a big explosive conflict. I came home one day and could hear my little two yelling from down the street. Their big brother had locked them outside of the house, barefoot, in the winter, and then denied it.

I walk from the kitchen to my car, and there's already yelling. I could not leave him home, even though he's the oldest, without some incident. So, when we had a babysitter come watch the little two, we sent him to a friend's house because most of the babysitters coming over were nearly his age.

So is this behavior genetic? Is it because of the adoption or early trauma? Would they have had these unique needs in their bio homes as well? Can we love and nurture it out of them? Or is this really just a reflection of our flawed parenting? Have we somehow caused these behaviors?

I'm never going to have the answers to all of these. But I want them. Even if it's my fault, I want to know.

I'm sure that it's a crazy concoction of all of it, varied from child to child.

I used to be a lot more on the "nurture" side of the nature versus nurture argument. Now I'm not so sure. With all of our nurturing, they still have mannerisms, habits, and patterns that are far more like bio family, even though some of these were never witnessed or experienced by my children in their bio homes. The older they get, the more they seem to "look" like their bio families in the decisions they make, the ways they think, and in how they respond to circumstances, in spite of how we've loved and steered them differently. Even though they've lived with us over half their lives now, there are still so many remnants of their genetic and early-family experiences that haven't been loved or nurtured out of them. The obsessive compulsive lying that characterizes his bio family, or her endless seeking after a father's approval in young men, even though she's had a loving, devoted father for the last seven years of her life... these things are the things we tuck away in wonder and, sometimes, in despair.

We wonder that after all the reshaping, and rewiring, and undoing we've tried to do... will it be in vain?

No. No it won't.

Because even if genetics are powerful. Even if those first five years of memories, subconscious or otherwise, overwhelm what we've been teaching them, I know something has gotten in. I know that we've done our part. At the very least, we've given them a life that has ruined them for their old ones. We've shown them the world, how vast and limitless and full of possibility it is. They can't go back to a slum, not for long, and find any contentment there. Because they've tasted better.

This is my hope for all of our kids. As delusional and disillusioned as they may be, they've now tasted better. They will always have a nagging conviction that they're settling for far less when they try to relive their parents' lives. This is my hope and my prayer. That the nurturing has made its mark, even if it hasn't remade the child. It will seal them for better things.

Opportunities they wouldn't have had or known about otherwise.

I can only guess at what's typical and what's trauma. But at the end of the day, whatever the reasons, these are my children and this is who they are. And my job is to keep trying, to keep pouring, to keep loving, even when I don't see the results I long for. And when we get a glimpse of the work our love has done, I cling to it. I write it down and share it and re-read it. Because they are few and far between, but they are there, like little markers of light and hope along the way saying, "See? Keep on keeping on."

You too, friend. Keep on. In the midst of all the questions and the unknowns and the black holes of why this kid is the way he or she is… keep on. Keep pouring. Keep investing. Keep trying. Even our mistakes are beautiful lessons of what it means to be human. We get up and try again…a skill they are going to need to learn and have in life. Who better to model it than us?

In the next two chapters, I will focus on the two aspects of parenting foster and adopted children that can be the most devastating and painful for us.

It is also, in my opinion, the least talked about subject. Let me rephrase that… it's the least honestly talked about subject: bonding and attaching, both us to them, and them to us. Not only have we had other people try to hold us to their version of "equality" in our family but also we often hold our own selves to a version of "attached" or "not attached." And we often work hard to present it one way to the public while really struggling in our own hearts.

I'm going to open that door. I will share with you my own heart-struggles in bonding and attaching, as well as some of the stories of other friends. And I will remind you, over and over, that you are not alone.

CHAPTER 17

The Challenge of Their Attachment

"It was a terrible division, to feel such need for someone, and yet angry that need existed."

— Robin Hobb, Ship of Magic

One of the terribly great struggles we've had in our adoption story is our experience with attachment and bonding.

First of all, let's talk about the difference between the two. I often hear people use the two words interchangeably (and I have been guilty of doing so myself) but they are actually quite different.

Bonding occurs in the first hours of life. It is the tie that a parent feels to this new human being in their lives. It's similar to imprinting. Think of a baby duck who decides that "mama" is the first moving object it spies, and who then follows it, regardless of whether it's a duck or not. Similar to imprinting, bonding is that sudden connection you feel to a child, especially upon first contact with the child immediately after birth. There are critical moments following birth in which these ties must be formed. Some will argue that if these opportunities are missed, the chance of ever forming a bond is minimal, affecting the well-being of the child forever.

This is not the case with attachment.

Attachment refers, instead, to the relationship between parents and child that develops gradually. And while, for some, attachment can happen quickly, it is never instantaneous. Sometimes I feel this for the little friends of my own younger children. I can feel connected and say that I love them. This has built over time, as I've come to know them and their families.

Attachment evolves over time, passing through important phases, drawing on the experiences of the preceding phases. Newborns aren't even capable of this kind of attachment, since they have little ability to distinguish between people or objects. "Because attachment refers to a relationship and not simply an experience of the parent, it is not appropriate to say that an attachment relationship has formed until the second half year [after six months]. Even then the relationship is not fully formed or fixed."[1] While those first hours and days are super important, so are the days and weeks and years that follow. Really, it's the quality of relationship that the child experiences over the history of care that determine how easily (or not) a child will find attachment with others later in life. "If the infant experiences consistent, dependable care that is responsive to his [her] signals and needs, he [she] will develop an abiding confidence in care and trust in self and others."[1]

The beauty of attachment is that while it isn't instantaneous, it's also not lost in those early days of life.

This is good news for those of us who weren't present at the birth of our children. Yes, we'll have some work to do in order to catch up, especially the older the child is, but it's not a fixed impossibility. Of course the odds are better the earlier you adopt.

There are situations in which a child will fail to attach later in life. For these children, special treatment may be necessary.

Children who've been raised in an institution without a parent figure, or even in a home with physically and emotionally neglectful parents, in those first six month of life, can struggle miserably with attachment later. Sadly, this is more and more common in many of the bio homes from which our children come.

For some, this means we need an even greater commitment to our adopted or foster kids.

For others, there is really nothing we can do but continue to love, pray, and seek the help available for our hard-to-attach kids. Their brains have wired around the neglect message of "You have to take care of yourself. Survival depends on you alone. Trust no one." And life in foster care or orphanages often reinforces the message, strengthening the brain's remapping. Every move in foster care proves it. Every change in schools proves it. Every disappointment proves it.

And then they come to us, fallible humans who will disappoint, and we end up proving it, too.

Even though it's not true.

One adopted teenager told me that he had purposefully never attached to his adopted family. I was surprised by his self awareness as he shared the memories of his birth family, though he left quite young, and the conflict in his heart that told him, if he attached to his adopted family, he was dismissing his birth family. He expressed regretting the choice and wishing that he could say "I love you" to his adopted family. He knows he's loved. He knows he was chosen. But his choice has been to not get close, to keep his distance and love from afar... and keep the connection he feels with his birth family. I don't know how many adopted children can put words to it as he does, but I'm grateful to be a friend in the struggle as he navigates this heart stuff.

I also think that sometimes being attached looks like unattached. As in the story I mentioned above, he wants to say, "I love you," because he DOES love them! He has kept his emotional distance, but their love and devotion to him has been loud and clear. Based on my conversation with him, I'd venture to guess that his parents don't feel close to him and wonder about the distance in their relationship. Yet, with an outsider, he communicated wishing that he was closer to them and regretting not expressing more love to his adopted family.

They come to us in a fog of psychological confusion. I explained my son to a coach one day and he said, "You're son is psychologically confused." He nailed it. That's exactly what he is. It's not just an identity hunt. It's confusion that is so deep and twisted inside that it traps him in a psychological and emotional cell. He wants to get out but doesn't know how. Even when we hand him the key, show him the lock on the door of his prison cell, and model walking in and out... he just looks at us dumbfounded.

I know you get this. When you've given them every opportunity, short of grabbing their bodies and guiding them through the motions of success (in whatever circumstance). We can't live their lives for them, so we give them every tool, show them how they work, and walk them through it. And still they look at us like they've never seen us before. Or the tool. Or the way out.

This is psychological confusion. They are stuck. They know they're stuck. And they have no idea how to get unstuck, even when we tell them how.

A friend recently shared that, as a child (and even young adult) she had a filter that translated everything into "you're going to leave me, too." She felt this same stuckness. As an adult, she can reflect on her childhood and adolescent years with clear eyes. She remembers how blind she was to the filter over her mind. She brought that filter into marriage, treating her husband like he had already left her, even though he was very loyal and faithful and had no intention of leaving. She wasn't aware at the time that she was treating him this way. Finally, after some great help, she was able to understand her actions and the reasons behind them.

But another interesting thing she realized was that, in her stuckness, in her own frustration and never getting it right, she would self-harm. But not in the way you might be thinking. She would finally just do something bigger and worse than usual in order to get the punishment she deserved. She brought on punishment to make herself pay for all the ways she just couldn't figure out how to live life well.

I see this in my children, I think. I see the roller coaster ups and downs and twists, and the occasional biggie that reels them in. They expect the punishment, and maybe part of them causes it in order to ease the sense of guilt and frustration over not being able to get it right. To return to the prison analogy, it's like our son is in his own prison, with every resource for getting out... but since he still can't figure out the key-in-the-hole bit, he begins to yell and scream and call us names. That way, we just leave him in there and he's "safe" but also getting what he deserves.

All of this makes me feel psychologically confused too!

It is so painful to have brought a child into your life, a child you've chosen to love, for whom you've sacrificed much, only to have them remain distant and unattached. I feel that every day. I do know that my son and daughter love us. And once or twice a year, it's evident in typical ways. Ways that we cling to the rest of the year when it's not there. When they're lying about our care to others. Ooh, this hurts me!

It hurts when I've laid down so much and then they tell people we've been neglectful or abusive or that we don't love them or want them. It hurts when, in their own anger and hurt, they lash out at the other children in our home. It hurts when they tell others how spoiled their little brother and sister are and how differently they're treated. It hurts deeply.

I had no idea that giving SO MUCH to a child, only to have them stab you in the back over and over, would be so painful. I guess I thought I'd remain noble and that my love was without needing reward. The lies that say we are the opposite of all we've been... they hurt. Then I can't wrap my brain around how to help these kids understand how loved they are. How wanted. How cherished and valuable. Because by now, sweet Jesus, they should know!

Oh boy, have I ever done this with God. I've been that child to whom He has shown such great kindness and love who then turns around and questions it all, begs for proof, even after all He's already done. This humbles me. And it strengthens me.

Maybe we're not so different after all, these kids and I.

---

1. Charles Nelson, "Early Report, Winter 1991, Attachment and Bonding," accessed October 10. 2015, www.cehd.umn.edu/CEED/publications/ earlyreport/earlyreportwinter1991.html

CHAPTER 18

❧❧❧

The Challenge of Our Attachment

❧❧❧

"I wondered how long it took for a baby to become yours, for familiarity to set in. Maybe as long as it took a new car to lose that scent, or a brand-new house to gather dust. Maybe that was the process more commonly described as bonding: the act of learning your child as well as you know yourself."

— Jodi Picoult, Handle with Care

I'm just going to say it.

I love all of my children.

And the love is different for each one.

The feelings of enjoyment change moment by moment, day by day.

Those feelings are not equal. I do not feel the same level of closeness with each child. I do not feel the same level of attachment.

And I'm not just talking about what I feel from them. I'm talking about what I feel *for* them.

I read a wonderful article, "A Different Kind of Love" by Kate Hilpern, looking at this very issue. It contains stories from adoptive parents and their feelings of love and connection with their children. Some parents said they felt an immediate connection, regardless of age. Others said they've never felt the same way toward biological kids as toward adopted. Some said they favored their adopted children (in action) because the relationship took so much intentionality. Others said they really struggled to even like their adopted child.[1]

I hear my story in these stories.

I hope you hear yours, too.

The article closed with a quote from Pam, a psychiatric social worker and an analytical psychotherapist: "I've worked with adopters who have been racked with guilt that they didn't have the same feelings for their adopted child. But that's all the more reason that we should stop this pretense that adopting is the same as having your own children. I'm not suggesting anyone should outline every detail of that difference to their children. That would be dire. But they do need to own the feeling and be OK with it."[1]

We have faced incredible pressure from people who've never adopted, to not show any inconsistency in what they perceive as "love" for our children. *WOW!* What if we did that to every parent? Went around as love-enforcers, pressuring them to love their kids exactly equally in the way WE perceive love? Absurd!

And yet there are people in my life who feel they have that patrol. They made comments on Facebook if too many pictures show up with only my biological kids (who, at the time, weren't school age yet and spent their entire day with me, while the older two were in school). They made comments if a family photo lacked one of the adopted kids (who, God forbid, could be the one behind the camera). But do they ask if one of my biological kids are missing from an event? A picture?

No.

I'm sure you've felt this pressure. Maybe some of the people in your circle aren't as loud about it as a couple of ours have been, but they're out there, passing comments that aren't entirely direct, but seem to be questioning the equality of your love.

Lord have mercy.

This only compounds the guilt and fear that I've already carried around for so long. I was under the impression, when we adopted, that I would feel exactly the same for all of my children, adopted or otherwise. That I would love them desperately, unconditionally, without rhyme or reason.

But for what other stranger does that really ever happen?

The reality is, I brought a handful of older children into my house. They were strangers. They didn't look like me. They didn't act like me. They hardly spoke my language. They didn't even smell like me.

That was one of the first things that struck me (and surprised me that I noticed). Still, my biological children, who are now eight and six, just smell like home. But my older two, even though they've been in our home as long as the little two, still carry their own distinct aromas. They always have (so it's not just puberty!).

This stands out to me because of what we know about the

sense of smell. We each have one thousand smell receptors in our nose. The odors that enter our nose either stimulate or inhibit these receptors. The receptors then signal our brain. It contributes 90% of what we taste. It's a life-saver…the reason pregnant women have such sensitivity to smell is (I believe) God's design to protect us from eating putrid food (especially in eras without refrigeration).

Our sniffers can distinguish between one trillion different odors, making our nose the most sensitive organ in its distinction of stimuli. Research has also shown that the memories we have associated with smells are the most powerful of our memories. In her 2007 article, "How Can Smell Change Your Decisions?" Robyn McMaster said, "The sense of smell is hard-wired deep into the brain's sensitive areas, that process emotion [amygdala], and, motivation and memory [hippocampus]."[2]

She also noted that mothers and their newborns recognize each other by scent.

I wonder if, even after all of these years, my children's biological mother could pull them in, take a deep breath, and still smell home.

In addition to the difference in aroma, we also had to be careful in the physical affection we showed (legally) our foster children. Already, at the age of eight, physical touch wasn't natural with a stranger's child, for them or us. My son has always responded with rigidity when we touch him. My daughter goes in and out of being very affectionate with my husband, but hardly at all with me.

But it's never felt awkward with the biological children. Or some of their friends. I'd say that from about three-years-old on down, I could easily grab a child and wrap them in my arms. I kiss my friend's one-year-old on the head. I stroke the heads of my little ones' friends. The touch is more natural... though it's never a question in my mind, with them, that I'm loving my friend's child as an auntie.

That's not the case with our adopted children. They are ours and we are supposed to show them undying love in all equality.

And yet, when my child spent his entire eight years with us lying, manipulating, stealing, and blaming us for everything he wouldn't take responsibility for, it's hard to be close. I wanted to enjoy him. I wanted a good relationship with him. But what other relationship in life are you forced to continue and be reprimanded for anything less when you are so mistreated? People divorce for lesser reasons. Friendships end for lesser reasons. Jobs are left for lesser reasons. And yet we are supposed to show to the world that how we feel about this person is no different than how we feel about the others who (mostly) interact with us affectionately, respectfully, with reciprocated love, with laughter, with touch.

It's a simple human experience, yet we demand more of ourselves because we've adopted them.

I do.

I've spent so much time feeling guilty and embarrassed and ashamed that I've had such different feelings for my kids. It's not even about who I birthed and who I didn't. Some days, they ALL irritate me! (And I'm sure I irritate them!).

What I've come to realize and embrace in my family story is that we are all different people. And I won't expect more of myself in this relationship than what is realistic. I won't force myself to pretend that I'm super close or connected to a child who rubs my name in the mud, continues to steal and hide, continues to reject our authority as parents. Do I love them? Absolutely. If I didn't, I wouldn't be bothered or hurt or affected by their actions. I wouldn't care about their future. I wouldn't keep trying.

I do love them.

But my love looks different. It feels different. My feelings of connection aren't even the same between adopted children. I feel differently for each one. Or between my biological children. Depending on the day of the week, the time of month, my mood, my day, and a whole host of other correlating factors, those feelings can go from joyful and close, to distant and detached. But underlying all of the fickleness of feelings is a love that runs deep. A love that, through all, hopes for the best. A love that hasn't given up.

I have given all that I can give and he has rejected much of it. I will continue to give of myself, but there is certainly some distance in my heart, as any person would have toward another who treats them in these ways. They're "kids." They're still learning and they're psychologically confused, and my love is not enough to heal that in them. I will continue to offer it, but I can recognize that, until they heal from their trauma, our relationship will feel the strain of our differences.

Hilpern says that "because today's adoptions often involve older children who come from backgrounds of neglect or abuse, they require what Jonathan Pearce, the director of Adoptions UK, calls therapeutic parenting. 'Of course, this is different to raising a biological child, just as it is different to raising an adopted child 30 or 40 years ago. It's parenting that I think should include on-going training, just as you have with any other demanding job,' he says. 'Does that mean the feelings are different? Yes, they are. Is the love any different? I just don't know. It will vary from one family to the next.'"[1]

I've spent so much time wondering what's wrong with me. Am I damaging my child because I feel this way in my heart? We've tried very hard to keep things as equal, by all appearances, as possible. Sometimes, I have to stop and ask myself, "What would I do if this were my biological child asking?" and often, I'm grateful to realize that my answers would be the same.

But every now and then, they would be different and I adjust my response accordingly. I want my children, all of them, to know that regardless of our struggles, our differences, our backgrounds... they are loved. Even when the relationship is strained, they are loved. Even when they lie and cheat and steal and manipulate, they are loved. It's not a fluffy love. It's not a love without consequence. But it IS love.

Because we haven't released them to the alternatives.

We love them.

Other Factors

I know it's not just their trauma that leads to this difficulty. We bring to this relationship our own baggage, issues, history and our own filters in which we view the world. Their stuff comes up against our stuff. Their personality comes up against ours.

My son, trauma aside, is an extreme extrovert. And now he's a teenager. He's working on actually being funny. My mom is so wonderful; she courtesy laughs all the time. It may not be funny, but she'll laugh just to make you feel good. I can't. It feels so deceptive. I wish I were more like her (able to laugh anyway). In her home, my son feels hilarious. We're just different.

I'm an introvert. I love my time alone. I need it to recharge.

I'm also type-A. I'm detail-oriented, I'm focused, I'm rational. I'm goal-driven. I love a good conversation. I'm linguistically gifted. I loved school and learning. I see a problem and I want to be part of the solution. These are all the things that my son is not. He's completely disorganized in every possible way. He's distracted, abstract, and pleasure-driven. He's impulsive. He's charming and gregarious and wins a crowd easily. He could be with people all day, every day. He doesn't see problems, only opportunities for pleasure, which he'll bring anyone along to join. He's a great person. But for all our differences, he may as well be from Mars. And I know he often feels the same way with me.

I felt this way with my mom a little, too. Though she and I aren't as extremely different, we struggled to understand each other. And I'm not adopted (though I thought I was for a while!). Living together was hard. But a little distance and the finishing steps in the development of my brain have led to a great relationship. We probably still shouldn't live together for very long...but I love her. I love talking to her. I miss her. I hope and pray this will be the story of my son and me as well, a little distance, a little brain development, and hopefully our attachment can build.

I know this is a hard chapter. It's hard to confront the dark places of our heart toward our kids. I hope that what you hear me saying, over and over, is that you are not alone. Not only are you not alone, but there are valid reasons for what you're feeling. They are legitimate. This is so freeing to me as I walk this journey. It lifts the burden of being something I can't be. I can't force my attachment to each child to feel the same. But I can embrace the love I have for them in their own unique ways. I can own that in this season of parenting some of my kids, the nature of their interactions with us causes me to pull back and feel the distance. And it's normal.

If you're reading this then you haven't given up. You haven't quit.

And that is love.

Keep Pouring

These words have stuck with me. A counseling colleague of mine encouraged me in this when I said, "I feel like I'm pouring and pouring into this kid and it all just seeps out the cracks."

"Your job is to keep pouring," he said. Keep pouring. Regardless of outcome, of your perception of success, of their response, of the circumstances… keep pouring. Keep giving and loving and showing up each day. Sometimes, my success was that I didn't say anything negative. Or I made an effort to make eye contact and ask about their day (even when I'd been dealing with emails and phone calls about them all day). Sometimes, it was enough that I got out of bed and made breakfast. Keep pouring.

1. Kate Hilpern, "A different kind of love," The Guardian, December 15, 2007, accessed October 10, 2015, www.theguardian.com/lifeandstyle/2007/dec/15/familyandrelationships.family

2. Robyn McMaster, "How Can Smell Change Your Decisions?" Brain Based Biz (blog), October 12, 2007, accessed October 10, 2015, www.brainbasedbiz.blogspot.com/2007/10/smell.html

CHAPTER 19

The Challenge of Family, Friends, and Community

*"We could see friends, family, and our church dropping like flies around us. No offers of dinners, no phone calls, no visits to check on us or check on these poor children......
I would have given my CAR for someone to sit and hold a crying baby just so I could shower! Laundry piled up, pantry was bare because I couldn't even get to the grocery store, too many doctors appointments to even count, I was losing my mind, and I looked around and no one was there. I felt abandoned. That was devastating."*

—Humans of Foster Care

A nother one of our greatest challenges in raising foster or adopted children is our own friends and community.

They are also some of our greatest resources for success and ease in parenting these kids.

Like all loved ones, this component of our parenting can have the greatest impact for harm or for good.

I'm a firm believer in the African saying, "It takes a village to raise a child." I believe we all need loving guidance, both in the way of encouraging as well as correcting, from the community around us. Ironically, the communities we view as "uncivilized" often live out this ideal the strongest.

In his book, The Long Walk to Freedom, Nelson Mandela wrote about family in his tribe of origin. "In African culture, the sons and daughters of one's aunts or uncles are considered brothers and sisters, not cousins. We do not make the same distinctions among relations practiced by Whites. We have no half-brothers or half-sisters. My mother's sister is my mother; my uncle's son is my brother; my brother's child is my son, my daughter."[1]

I have found a movement in American culture (at least in my circles) to family-ize our closest friends. My children have multiple "aunts" and "uncles" who aren't blood relation, but were probably supposed to be. And I am "Aunt Marcy" to a handful of my best friends' children as well. Whether you do this or are opposed to it, the point is, we're making our way back to bringing people into our "tribe" and raising our kids together.

But suddenly, when we adopt or foster, we can feel like a mother duck raising kittens (thanks Linda, for the analogy!). The community we have in place may have a hard time understanding what we've done. They often struggle to understand how foster and adoptive kids are not raised in the same ways. Don't respond to the same parenting tricks. Don't have the history and immediate bond that comes with birthing them. We're only figuring it ourselves, so, of course, they don't get it!

Even so, the best of the best will come alongside us, taking their "auntie" or "uncle" role with all its meaning, and embrace whomever we call son or daughter. These are the people to cling to. I mean, not in a psychotic, never-leave-me kind of clinging. But these are the people to take care of. To keep close. To love and cherish and intentionally commit to your flock of support and respite. And it probably goes without saying, but offering the same in return, within your ability, is crucial. No one wants to be the rescuer of someone who never gives back. But if you're like me, the gift of their love and time and support will overwhelm your soul, and it will be all you can do to contain it. Giving back won't be hard.

When we began fostering, we only knew two other people who'd adopted. One was in our community and had adopted newborns privately. The other was a single Canadian woman who'd fostered, then adopted, a number of ethnically different children while she was working on her Masters degree. But other than that, no one.

Our church wasn't really sure what to do with us at first. But heck, neither were we. The gift was how willing they were to figure it out alongside us. Eventually, we adopted some new rules, standards, and precautions. We had bio parents show up looking for kids. We had rules and legalities that were foreign to church friends… like needing social worker permission for a sleepover or a field trip with the youth group. And though we all got bumps and bruises, we did it. And they did it with us.

*A note here: any kind of "institution" welcoming foster families (and adoptive families) will need some educating and some hard conversations. I knew a couple of people who had Sunday School childcare workers call Child Protective Services on the family! I understand the laws of mandated reporting (I've been a mandated reporter for most of my working life) however our kids often spin tails for attention. And in at least one of these instances, the reporter only heard some of the interaction between mother and foster daughter, but when she called CPS, she embellished the situation to fill in the gaps.

The tragedy of the situation is multifaceted. For one, all the mother really needed was some help. That childcare worker could have come around the corner and offered a helping hand instead of eavesdropping behind a wall (leaving her Sunday school class unattended) in order to have a reason to call. Secondly, reports like that, even when they come back unfounded (as they often do) remain on a person's record. Sure, they'll tell you over at CPS that it won't affect you, but it will.

One friend and her family can't house an exchange student just because calls were made, even though they were all unfounded. I'm not saying don't call if there's suspicion of abuse. But I would expect, especially in a church, that the members would live out the call of Christ to serve and love others and have a conversation with the family before taking such life-changing steps against them.

Let's help our families, not hurt them. I imagine this could end up being a huge reason that families who adopt or foster would avoid church. And that's a tragedy also... because what better community than the ones with a built-in mandate to care for orphans in their distress!

We need support. We don't need any help being torn down; we get enough of that from the System. We get the constant surprises we're faced with, the guilt we put on ourselves for all of the fears, the embarrassment, the confusion, the doubt.

We definitely don't need anyone to look for a reason to stomp us. We don't need unsolicited advice from people not raising children of trauma. We don't need people looking for ways they think we don't love our children equally and pointing it out. We don't need people to make assumptions about our fertility, our motivations for fostering or adopting (PLEASE, it is NOT for the money... they couldn't afford the work this takes, and we would have done it for free if we could have afforded it).

We don't need questions about our "real" kids (like the others are "unreal) or our "natural" kids (as if the others are "unnatural") or even our "chosen" kids (as if the others were unwanted or unchosen). Yes, it's different but unique in their own ways. We don't need comparison charts on how someone feels about raising bio children and how it should be the same for us. We don't need people assuming our kids are wild because they've been adopted or being so surprised that they're well-behaved (in spite of being adopted). We don't need people to jump on their phone with CPS before even getting to know us, our family, or, really, our children. We don't need to be ostracized, talked about, or turned away.

And really, we don't even need anyone to tell us how amazing we are because they could never do this.

Trust me, we don't feel amazing.

What we DO need are friends who, even though they may not be living it, are willing to trust us, to listen, to join in and to stick around long enough to see it for themselves. Because, oh boy, our kids won't hide it from you for very long if you're in our house a while.

We DO need people to celebrate our new arrivals with baby-shower type events. Celebrate the new lives! It's not always about the gifts, it's about community coming together and acknowledging and praising this new family member.

We DO need people to help us with meals sometimes, just like you would with a new birth. A meal means SO much to a family struggling to drive kids to five therapy appointments a week, doctors appointments, visits with bio family, meetings with social workers, school, and whatever else they ask us to fit in.

We often feel alone, out of place, and lost. We DO need you to bring us into your circle and include us, to be willing to learn with us how to be together with this kid who sometimes says the wrong thing, does the wrong thing, throws major tantrums on the floor. Just be there. Hug us. Smile. Keep inviting us.

We DO need people who will listen to our story and share theirs. We love it (unless it's a really bad day) when people express interest in fostering and adopting.

We DO need people who, when they say that want to support us and be respite for us, follow through when the need arises. It means the world to us when someone who says they'll help, actually does.

We DO need friends to check in with us. We might have a smile plastered to our faces, too embarrassed to share how hard this is. Send a text, an email, a phone call, just to see how we're doing. How we're REALLY doing. We need space to cry and process and find our grounding again.

And we need naps. If you can take our kids for a couple hours, we could learn to breath again. We can recharge and get ready for the next episodes of putting out fires. You have no idea how much a few hours (or days) away from our kids means to our sanity. I'm not kidding. That's just my reality.

It doesn't mean I don't love my kids.

Actually, it means I do. Because I'm not willing to force us through a situation we aren't equipped to handle well.

We all need that kind of grace with ourselves, the grace to be gentle with ourselves. And to ask for gentleness from others.

1. Nelson Mandela, Long Walk to Freedom: The Autobiography of Nelson Mandela, (London, England: Little, Brown, and Company, 1994), 9.

CHAPTER 20

The Challenge of the Transient Life

"To love at all is to be vulnerable. Love anything and your heart will be wrung and possibly broken. If you want to make sure of keeping it intact you must give it to no one, not even an animal. Wrap it carefully round with hobbies and little luxuries; avoid all entanglements. Lock it up safe in the casket or coffin of your selfishness. But in that casket, safe, dark, motionless, airless, it will change. It will not be broken; it will become unbreakable, impenetrable, irredeemable. To love is to be vulnerable."

—C.S. Lewis

One of the greatest challenges in fostering specifically (though some adopted children also relate to this) is the transient lifestyle. This is a challenge that pulls heavily on our own heartstrings. It's not a challenge of such physical effort or the busyness related to taking in more children, but the journeying with kids who may only be with us for a short time. It's the challenge of loving kids who've had so much change in their lives, they are further wounded beyond their initial trauma when they move on.

No matter how hard parenting them is, we do love them. We want the best for them. Even if we sometimes agree that the best may not be our house. Even when we see their biological families pull it together and reunite... we rejoice, and we weep. (Though I've sent at least one kid off with more rejoicing than weeping!)

The transient nature of their lives is hard. It's hard on them. It exacerbates their already deeply embedded fear of abandonment. It affirms their brain's decision to rewire for survival. Every time they move, they lose something. They lose actual things, like belongings that the foster home didn't pass along. But they also lose another notch on their trust meter.

And so do we, right? We hope to adopt but they get moved instead.

When we watch the broken system return them to a broken home, a piece of our hearts goes with them but our hands are tied. We have to let go... even when, on the inside, we're screaming at the injustice, and we're wracked with fear about what will become of this child.

And sometimes, we see them again... back in the system, more broken than before. And that brokenness only makes them harder to parent, so over and over, they are passed along. We watch from the sidelines. We wonder from our homes.

I've known families to be devastated to have to release the children they love into horrible situations, only to be proven right later. Devastated. My heart breaks for two little (not so little anymore) boys whom we still love, even though it's over time and distance. They were victims of a broken family and a broken system. Their story in the stuff novels are written about. And now, with the gift of social media, I'm able to see what's become of at least a couple of them.

We've always told the kids who've come through that once they are our family, they are always our family. Even if an adoption never occurred. We've had kids stay in touch with us years after they've left. We've never had to ask for a child to be removed, which I'm grateful for. In their minds, we were never the "bad" guys who gave up on them. We're not angels. We just found that right when we were at our limit… an outside factor would lead to their removal to another placement.

Of the seven kids we fostered, we adopted two. Of the remaining five, one is in a really great adoptive home. She has a million special needs but is loved and cared for by a beautiful soul. One of our former foster children is dead. Rumor has it, she was accidentally killed in domestic violence. Two of the others are in gangs, drug and alcohol addicted, sexually promiscuous, and living out the same patterns of the biological family. We've lost contact with the last one but I keep waiting. Hoping. Praying that he's made his way.

This isn't everyone's story. But it is ours. And we continue to reach out and love these kids, even over the distance and time.

We've had our goodbyes. Some of our greatest fears going into foster care and adoption are that our hearts would be broken.

And that fear is often a reality. The director of our Foster Family Agency would say that means we're right for the job… these kids don't need robots to love them, they need caring people. People whose hearts can be broken, because it's really the love that makes them breakable.

Without love, we'd be stone and unaffected by our kids and their hard stories.

But we're not. Even on our worst days, we want to see them healthy and well and secure in love.

Even on my worst days, when I'm looking for my hideaway rock and I'm battling regret... un-adopting never crosses my mind. Because the alternatives for my child are not better than the difficulties we face now. And we've been offered some alternatives! But they aren't best for him. So I keep beating my head against the wall, hoping for a change in him, a change in me, a change, but not just any change. Not a detrimental change. Not a harmful change. Just a comfortable one. And it comes in small moments, fleeting moments, but they come. And they give me hope that one day they will come and stay.

When They Want to Stay

You've become all they know. Their safe place. It's taken time. Hard work. So Much Work. You've been all in.

And then they get sent back to their biological families. And the social worker comes, and they're clinging to your knees. Begging, crying, pleading to stay. And maybe you're crying too, but you want to be strong. You want to believe that this is best, that they'll be okay. And they're pulled away, arms outstretched, screaming for you.

You have so many words you want them to hear, to imprint on their minds and hearts. That they are loved. That this is not rejection. That this is not your choice. And that this can be good. That you'll stay in touch, if you can. Hopefully you can. But you probably can't. They get buckled in, kicking and crying. The door closes and the car pulls away, leaving you with their tear-stained faces, confusion and betrayal written all over them.

And you fall apart.

Because the stresses of change and goodbyes are not only theirs. They are ours too. Fostering and adopting don't only begin with loss... it is the common thread all the way through.

We step into a world of the deepest pains and grief when we choose to love these children. We take on their hurt and we hurt too. This is why so many people tell us, "I could never do what you do… it would hurt too much."

It *should* hurt. Sending away a child you love should hurt. Loving hurts.

There is a cost to caring.

And if we spend our lives avoiding hurt, then we also choose to avoid the most beautiful and precious gifts in life:

The chance to love another.

The chance to see radical healing among the broken.

The chance to be a part of transformation in the lives of others.

The chance to develop a deeper character and heart for the world.

The chance to be loved by the least loved.

The chance to *feel*. We have so numbed ourselves by constant stimulation: business, Internet, TV shows… we've numbed the pleasure centers of our brains because it's safe. It doesn't hurt. Or does it?

The pain of goodbye is in the loving. The really loving. The risk-taking. The plunge into a world that involves pain, yes, but also indescribable joy.

If anything makes us brave, it is this.
That we looked pain in the face, knowing it was our great fear, and stepped in. But not unarmed. We stepped

in, knowing that love would be our guide... and that a life without love is a pointless life.

We've chosen meaning. Purpose. Something greater than ourselves.

That's why we're willing to be hurt. Because we were first willing to love.

This is beautiful, friends.

I believe that even the deep frustration I feel in raising my oldest two is birthed from a love for them. This love looks different than what I expected, but it is love. It's a love that's willing to do this every day, over and over, with the hope that they will be better for it, somehow, someway.

I don't always recognize this as love. And I'm sure they don't always either.

But it is. Because there is no greater love than to lay down one's life for one's friends (or strangers, in our case). (John 15:13)

The Community Goodbye

Sometimes we forget that our goodbye is also our community's goodbye. Our friends and family who've walked alongside us, invested in our children, and been intentional with their support... they grieve the loss of our child, too.

They may not show it in the same way.

And for some, their grief will look like abandonment. They'll shy away from the pain and guard their hearts for a while. This feels like a double wound for us sometimes... to see friends and family walk away to avoid being hurt again. But we understand it a little, don't we? Sometimes, we're not so quick to dive back in ourselves.

They're hurting.

But I think they don't give themselves as much permission to hurt, because they were "just" the friend or "just" the teacher or "just" the whatever. They weren't the parent, so they should suck it up.

But they do hurt. And they should. They loved this child, too.

In the midst of our own grief, let's try to be aware of the ways our people are hurting also. The ways that they are dealing with this loss in their lives also. Just as you would be pained if a dear friend's child passed away... so are they grieved when we lose one of our own.

This won't always look pretty. Grief is a mysterious creature. Some of us cry. Some of us yell. Some of us need something or someone to blame. Some of us hide behind big walls to keep from hurting again. Some of us dismiss our pain, stuffing it down and denying it a place in our heart or mind. Some of us embrace it and weep and wail and lament the full course. Some of us just get really, really angry.

My grief is often quite personal. I try to stay strong for my friends, to be a shoulder to cry on, to be an encouraging smile. And then I break down on my own, away from the crowd. I'm sure I appear quite unmoved and stoic at times to others... but I'm holding it together, waiting for my turn. And when my turn comes, look out. I'll be a mess, a private mess, but a mess all the same. Sometimes, I can't keep it in and the mess starts to leak out with my people, and I'm learning to let it.

Permission to Grieve

I'm sure grief looks different for you, as well. As we grieve the goodbyes, let's be full of grace for ourselves and for our people. Let's give them permission to process the loss, too. Let's at least acknowledge it. And let's grieve with hope. Let's believe that something beautiful can come from these ashes.

We need each other. We need to process our worlds. We need to be loved and we need to extend that love to the others hurting in our circles.

It's all messy.

But it's a beautiful mess.

CHAPTER 21

The Challenge of Identity

"Define yourself radically as one beloved by God. This is the true self. Every other identity is illusion."

— Brennan Manning, Abba's Child:
The Cry of the Heart for Intimate Belonging

Most of us go through some sort of identity seeking, especially during our adolescent years. It's something we as humans are always trying to sort out. In fact, our current Western culture is riddled with grown adults seeking an identifiable niche in life (while forcing everyone else to accept it). I can only imagine this hot pursuit of permission to be who you are is much less about everyone else accepting it and more to do with the individual's own journey of acceptance. Somehow, if society accepts you, then you can too, right? It's everywhere right now.

We have a woman, Rachel Dolezal, who, though born Caucasian, has been identifying herself as African American, even going so far as altering her appearance, disconnecting from her nuclear family, and claiming African American friends as her actual parents.

We have Caitlyn Jenner bringing to the forefront her identification with the female gender, though born male. This has now become a reality TV show.

My friend's daughter just started college. On her application were fifteen gender options. FIFTEEN! If that seems like a lot, Facebook gives you fifty-eight options for gender, and if you don't find yourself on that list, no worries… you can customize your gender entry.

Clearly, Westerners seem to be still working on their own identities.

So why are we so surprised when our adopted and foster kids do too? I guess it's not the surprise that they will, it's how they go about it. Each kid is so different from the next. And sometimes, during the hunt for their identity, they reject us… either for a time or forever. More often, though, they come back around. But still, after all the hardship, to have them say we aren't good enough is devastating. And even though we've heard from others that this moment might happen, when it does, it's heartbreaking and infuriating.

We've known that our kids would one day want to know their biological families. Why wouldn't they? I would want to know. At least to see my face in someone else's or have some questions answered. We hoped to have the time to raise our kids to a level of maturity before opening that door for them.

Their interest has changed over the years. At first, for one of them, there was fear. He was afraid they would find him and try to kidnap him, as they've done with some of their other children. He was afraid that once again he'd be the victim of his parents' malicious and destructive behavior. That he'd again bear the consequences of their addictions, their dissoluteness. But this has now changed to curiosity. The problem is that their families are still really, really dysfunctional. They are not healthy people. Their patterns rage on. But now we feel more greatly the tension between our kids' desire to know more and the danger lurking behind that door.

These kids are often overwhelmed by the differences between themselves and their adopted family. They look for that connection somewhere. And if we don't provide a way, they'll find one somewhere. People are found relatively easily on the Internet. And if they don't go that route, they may look for identity in their peers, in drugs or alcohol, in gangs. Like all of us, they long to belong. A sense of self and a place in the world. Though we've given them one, there's always a hole. A small piece that keeps them discontent.

Lillian's daughter is turning seven. She was adopted at birth. For several years, she's been talking more about her birth mom. Where is she? Why did she give me up? Name? Picture? She cries for her birth mother and says she misses her. Even at seven, this sweet girl is looking for the pieces of her that feel missing. What's ironic is that Lillian and her daughter share enough similarities in their features, that people would never guess she's adopted. But still, something in her longs for this missing piece of her puzzle.

Even when or if they meet their bio families, there's often still a sense of not fitting in.

Many kids find this in their faith. And many kids find this in their adoptive families. It's not every adopted or foster child's story to seek their identity in other places, but it's hard to know how ours will handle it.

So we do our best, right? We make decisions that we think are the best for them. We read the articles. We try to learn about their culture and history and include it in their upbringing. Because that's what the articles will say to do.

But Mary Lou and her husband were still surprised. They

didn't realize that their kids would reject their birth country and culture as much as they did. In their pre-adoption training, the social workers talked so much about preserving their child's birth heritage, but they never mentioned that their children might absolutely refuse to speak the language, eat the food, look at pictures, or even talk about their country. "It's taken years for them to see past their hurt and begin to appreciate Ethiopian culture," she said.

Laura, on the other hand, was raised with two siblings adopted from South America. One of the siblings grew up to reject all things from her birth country. She refused to learn the language, to go visit the country, or even to interact with her discovered bio family.

Her brother, on the other hand, fully immersed himself in his birth culture. He learned Spanish, met his bio family, and has made multiple trips. He even changed his last name back to his birth name. Not as a slight to his adoptive family, he assured, but because he wanted to identify as that nationality. Two biological siblings, adopted into the same family, with such drastically different responses to their culture of origin.

Sometimes, when kids are in elementary school, their adoption is embarrassing. All they want is to fit in, and being adopted is something that distinguishes them from the rest. So they keep it quiet and do their best to fit in. These same kids, however, in their teen years, often want to stand out, to be unique and different. At this point, being adopted can become a "cool" thing and is embraced in a new way.

Even so, as a mother of two adopted teenagers, I find that my kids gravitate toward other adopted teenagers. And I totally get it.

It's the same reason I want other adoptive parents around me. They remind me that I'm not alone. They understand what I'm going through without the verbose explanation. Or any explanation. Even if our experiences are totally different, we become family just by nature of having journeyed a similar journey.

I bet this is true for my kids, too. I don't blame them. In fact, it means they bring their friends home and I get to hang out with *them* too. To hear their stories. Watch them navigate this identity thing. Encourage them from the sidelines. Join *their* parents in loving these kids. Because it really does take a community. And I'm all about being part of your community if it helps lighten the load.

Because that day might come when they turn away from us, when they project the cause of their trauma onto us or when, just by nature of being teenagers, they decide we're dumb and their friends are smarter (okay, that day has already come). And I pray that they will turn to you. To other parents who are on my team who get it, who can love them, embrace them, and enjoy them in all the ways they won't let me... or in the ways I can't.

And I will try to do that for you.

My husband, though not adopted, was born to the daughter of German and Danish immigrants, and the son of African-Colombian Caribbean parents. He was raised between countries. He spent much of his life looking for his place in the world, and never quite finding it. He tried religions, cults, relationships, addiction... and still always turned up empty.

Finally, after over thirty years of seeking, he found his identity in Jesus Christ. He found a place of unconditional belonging, regardless of color or language or gender and he didn't have to force it to happen. He discovered his place as a child of God, dreamed up, created, radically loved, sacrificially saved. Every other aspect of identity paled in comparison.

This is my hope for our children, too.

That they will find themselves in the love of God, children of a trustworthy Father, never abandoned, unconditionally loved, welcomed, sought, regardless of the choices they make, realizing their great need for Him. And everything else will pale.

This search for identity isn't really just about their identity, is it? Isn't it also about our family identity? And how much it shifts with each new child, each new need, each new issue?

We were once a traditional family. Okay, it only lasted for three months, but still. That's what we were. Now we're an adoptive family. My biological kids are already this strange mix of my husband's African-Colombian-Danish-German self and my Italian-Native American-Yankee self. Then we add my adopted kids with his Filipino-Mexican-American self and her Mexican-American self and who the heck are we?

Are we a White family? Are we a blended family? Are we an ambiguous family? Now we live in Germany. So we are all of these things living in a very caucasian country. These are just ethnic dynamics of our family. What about the way our genetics or personalities or ancestry or (fill in the blank) come into play? Who are we then?

Many families are surprised that the identity issues become family-identity issues as much as adopted-child identity issues. And when this surprise catches us, we jump into hyper reactive mode. We find ourselves surprised at what this all means for us. Who am I in this situation.

As a woman and mother, I find that society is quick to judge mothers. We have to face the world every day, knowing that people will judge us by this child's behavior. They will come to conclusions and make assumptions and, at the end of it all, something about them will be our fault. And maybe, sometimes, it is... but boy, isn't there a whole host of other correlating factors for who they are? Especially in our situations.

We know this, but we carry it all the same. We carry their judgments. We wonder if maybe it is our fault. Could we have loved them better? Poured into them more? Yelled less? Regretted less? Hugged more? Maybe, just maybe, this is hard because we've *made it hard.*

Oh, mama-friend, let me draw you in and say it isn't so. You can't carry that. I can't carry that. Maybe it's all true that we could have been more lenient and less harsh... but they choose their response. I choose my response. That's all I can carry: my part. Don't carry more than what's yours.

I'm not saying it isn't hard fathering these kids. I'm not a father but I live with one, and I walk this journey alongside him EVERY DAY. I've SEEN the difficulty. I've witnessed the awkward questions he gets asked. The awkward roundabout ways people try to say, "Why are you so hard on that child?" when they have NO IDEA how hard that child is on us.

My husband is a gifted teacher. He often stresses over our child's slander and the possible loss of credibility he has in our community as an educator. He worries that he will lose his job because of what our child claims in attention-seeking. He worries that people will finally realize that *we aren't perfect parents.* That we've adopted these kids and then made mistakes along the way.

Dads, you can't carry this either. My husband has found solace in this: God is our defense. He will bring about the truth. It may not happen in our timeframe, but we've seen it happen in our lives. When we've chosen not to argue, defend, convince... the truth comes out anyway. Our choices in character and integrity prove themselves.

We are always tempted to fight to protect our image to the community and to our own selves. We react. We defend. We try to convince ourselves and others that we're not as bad as they must be thinking we are. Because sometimes, we think they're all staring at us... but they're not.

And we can get caught up in this reactionary self-defense of all we've given, all we've sacrificed, all we've done. And it may be true, but it doesn't help.

We need to be healthy, not just for our sake, but for theirs. A healthy family equals a healthy child. Or at least a greater probability of a healthy child.

Here are some ways to wade through our own identity crisis:

Celebrate Your Family

Find ways to celebrate the uniqueness that is your family. Find ways to honor it. And do it with people who get it. Remember together the good things that have happened, the progress made, the improvements you've all seen, the ways you've each grown.

Become a Student of History and Culture

Even though your child may end up rejecting their birth nation/culture, you don't have to. Learn everything you can about where they've come from. Do it for yourself if not for them.

Offer Access to Answers

Helping them connect with their past, reunite with meaningful people, and find pictures or family stories will show that you are available for this part of their journey. Many kids are afraid their questions will hurt their adoptive parents' feelings. Be preventative and let them know you've got the answers when they're ready. Or if you don't have answers, that you're willing to help get some.

CHAPTER 22

The Challenge of Birth Family

"Family was even a bigger word than I imagined, wide and without limitations, if you allowed it, defying easy definition. You had family that was supposed to be family and wasn't, family that wasn't family but was, halves becoming whole, wholes splitting into two; it was possible to lack whole, honest love and connection from family in lead roles, yet to be filled to abundance by the unexpected supporting players."

— Deb Caletti, The Secret Life of Prince Charming

It would be enough stress and struggle if we only had to battle the System or the surprises that come our way or the many aspects of parenting or our friends and community… But we also have to battle our fears.

I have to battle my fears.

My fear that my kids will one day grow up and return to their families of origin... who, in our case, are not healthy people. I fear that all of our work, our love, our sweat and tears, and pain will be washed away, and they'll fall into the same devastating habits and patterns and decisions as the ones who came before them.

Or I fear that they'll be like me. Because somewhere in the day to day of raising them and pushing through the challenges, I have lost the best me, the me who was selfless and humble and patient and kind. She pops up sometimes, but they've seen her ugly twin more often than not.

I fear that one day, their bio families will find them, reach out, and we'll lose them.

Or they will show up on the porch and want to see them or on the street and just take them.

Who are these people we fear? Who are the faces and names behind "bio" family? They are more than egg and sperm donors, though I've heard some refer to them as such. They are forever a piece of our children, intertwined now with our lives and families in a way that will never be undone. No amount of secrecy, of protection, of guardedness will change that.

We can die never having met them, and still, they will have influenced, impacted, and changed the course of our lives forever, for better or worse. These are mothers and fathers and sisters and brothers. They're aunts and uncles and cousins and grandparents. They are generations of people, who at this time, in this place, have been severed from one another... yet not completely. Threads bind them.

And now they bind us, too.

Louisa Leontiades, a now-grown adopted child, speaks to the reality of both "real" mothers in her life when she says, *"The relegation of my first real mother to the function of incubator by using the terms 'birth or biological mother' objectifies her, and diminishes her role and her importance in my heritage. She is also my 'real' mother plain and simple... I bonded with her before I was born during my very formation; she is and forever will be a part of me and I of her. And you—adopter—you are my parent. Maybe you are my 'real mother' too. After all, it's just a label. Two women played a part in making me who I am. My mother doesn't parent me. You do. Does this mean that either one of you is less important than the other? No. Without my mother, I would not be alive. Without you, I would not have survived to see adulthood. I would not be able to survive without either of you."* [1]

The language we use and are comfortable with varies from family to family. I tend toward "bio family," though when I read the words of Louisa above, I understand the objectification she points out. I think it's true. And it helps me.

In many ways, it helps me to objectify my children's former families. This is honest. And I'm not saying it's right or good. But I can't understand the choices they've made outside of this label... the choices they made which led to the removal of their children (in our case), the choices they made which forever severed their parental rights, and the choices they made to abduct some of their children after their legal rights had been terminated. Did this termination make them any less family? No. The blood and genes and DNA are still strong. It's still something they share that we don't.

I just can't imagine choosing drugs or alcohol or my own insecurities or lusts over my children. And thus, they are the "bio family" to me. The mysterious "them"—the unpredictable, hard to understand, distant, unsafe, cause of all that's hard in our lives.

Except that they're not.

But they're easy to blame, aren't they? But that's why they're so scary, right? Because we're afraid of what we don't know. Well, I'm also afraid of what I do know about them and how little I understand them by these decisions. But these things are mostly hearsay, with the evidence manifested in my children's behavior and brain-trauma.

The thing is, bio families aren't always the bad guys. Some of them are actually heroes... choosing life for their kids when they could have chosen death. Sacrificially handing their children over to better care than they could give. I have friends who are raising children because the birth parents knew that a child would suffer within their lifestyle. Or that they couldn't provide the best, so they chose another family. A gift.

Others lost their children against their will and tried really hard to do what they needed to do in order to get them back. But they just couldn't keep it together. They lacked resources or self-control. They were beat before they started.

One biological mother I knew was illiterate. She relied on her daughter (who was removed) to read all of the important documents and help her sign on the appropriate lines. She couldn't function at ALL in the system that required her to navigate public transportation in a big city, on a tight time schedule, while unemployed and uneducated. Add to it that she was developmentally delayed. She was more of a child in the home than a mother... but she loved her kids deeply in the way she knew how. She was born into this and didn't know any better. We helped her the best we could, but she wasn't able to do the bare minimum on her own.

We've watched (and walked with) a variety of bio families. All of my initial work in Social Services was with these families. These faces remind me that they are real people. Broken people.

There are also the parents who give all bio parents a bad name. The ones they write books about. The ones who chase their children around with drug needles, trying to poke them for sport. The prostitute mothers and the pimp fathers. The dads who bring their friends over to rape any of the girls who happen to be in the house, whether they're daughter, sister, friend.

The ones who, for five bucks, lose their rights to three of their children. The ones who have ALL of their fifteen kids in the system, somewhere, somehow: foster care, group homes, jails, prison. They are the liars, the slanderers, the child-abductors. They are the families whose memories alone trigger such trauma in a child that all the hard work seems to come undone at a smell, a season, a food. Any unsuspecting trigger and our kid is in pieces.

We have a kid from a home like this.

And I can't wrap my mind around it.

Can't bring myself to un-objectify them. The monsters who brought innocent lives into the world only to destroy them in the most horrific ways.

Most of these kids are ruined. One is dead.

A new generation of children being removed thanks to gangs, drugs, and alcohol… the family legacy of the lost and defeated.

So yeah, sometimes it's scary to think that they might want back in. Like a black fog pushing at the door, faceless but deadly. Yet I know that, one day, my kids will need to go back. To look into the faces that resemble theirs. And I pray that they will be mature and steadfast enough to let go of the fantasy they've held onto for years and see the truth of where they're from with compassion and with the sadness and mourning it deserves.

And then break the cycle.

I want them to be cycle-breakers. I'm raising them to be ruined for the lives they've been taken from. To have tasted better and not ever again be able to find satisfaction in less.

But I also want them to love, to make their peace with their stories. Their stories are messy... and they make mine messy now, too, but there can be so much beauty in the mess. That one day, years down the road, the beauty gets real. And I pray for healing and health and recovery for the bio families in our lives.

Because, like it or not, my kids have two mothers and two fathers. They may never see the former again, but they're here, always with us, always part of our family. They show up in their personalities. They show up in the shape of their eyes, the turn of their nose, the frames of their bodies. They show up in mannerisms and language. They show up in conversations, in dreams, in Facebook searches, in emails to the county that you find in their "sent" folder. They will always be a part of our lives.

Embracing this and preparing for it has lessened the stress of trying to block my kids from every possibility. We still filter and guard, but we also anticipate the day when we have to let them go... and trust that they'll know where home is.

---

1. Louisa Leontiades, "Five Hard Truths About Adoption Adoptive Parents Don't Want to Hear," Huffington Post, Last modified 09/01/2015, accessed October 10, www.huffingtonpost.co.uk/louisa-leontiades/five-hard-truths-about-ad_b_6131124.html

CHAPTER 23

୶ଡ଼ଵ

The Challenge
of Our Birth Children

ଵଡ଼ଵ

"Your children are the greatest gift God will give to you, and their souls the heaviest responsibility He will place in your hands. Take time with them, teach them to have faith in God. Be a person in whom they can have faith. When you are old, nothing else you've done will have mattered as much."

— Lisa Wingate, author

One of our great concerns and fears in raising adopted children was for our own birth children. Would the impact on them be detrimental? Or would they become better for it? Though our hearts were full of desire to be a part of the foster kid solution... this could be a deal-breaker. We wanted to hear thoughts from other biological children on the affects of being raised alongside foster and adopted children.

During our certification process, we were invited to a Christmas dinner for all of the foster families with our agency. It was wonderful. Many of the kids stood up and performed a talent. It was a room full of the most beautifully blended families. A decorated Christmas tree enriched the holiday atmosphere. I don't remember the food. I don't remember the names of everyone we met that night.

But I do remember the teenage daughter of one of the foster parents who stood and shared how meaningful it had been to be raised alongside foster kids. She talked about the years she'd spent sharing her room with foster kids who'd come and go, but how she'd come to love each one and saw them as a brother or sister. She missed them when they left and tried to stay in touch. She talked about how it has opened her eyes and heart to the stuff other kids go through in life and made her appreciate what she had.

This teenage girl spoke straight to our hopes and dreams for our own biological children that they would grow with these same eyes and hearts and love. She won us over, and we said, "Yes."

People suggested that we wait until our little kids were older. We spoke with kids who'd been raised with foster or adoptive kids and all had been older when the children were introduced. And all said it worked out well that way.

But we didn't want to wait fifteen years before helping kids.

So, when our birth son was three-months-old, we received our first foster child. He was supposed to be just a weekend respite... but he's now our sixteen-year-old son. (That's how that goes, right?). Six kids and seventeen months later, our second child was born. Exactly a month before her birth, we welcomed a little eight-year-old girl. She'd been my husband's student for two years and was now coming in as foster daughter. She's now our second oldest, our fifteen-year-old daughter.

Honestly, even though there are seven to nine years between the older and younger children, it often feels like we're raising four little people. Our older two had some developmental and emotional delays. There were times when my firstborn would develop a new cognitive function, and my oldest would grasp the same skill a few days or a week later. Even now, with teenagers and elementary-aged kids, there are still some major deficits. My oldest is charming and gregarious and *looks* sixteen, and by all outward appearances, should be expected to do sixteen-year-old things, both academically and socially. But that's just not his or our reality. If you were in the room right now, I'd grab you by the shoulders, look you in the eyes, and say, "THIS is so hard!"

So now, we are raising young children while our oldest are going through their teenage years. Now, mind you, teenage years aren't easy for anyone, are they? This would naturally be difficult enough. I think of the torture I put my parents through... oh man. And I was as biological as you get, and all full of teenage hormone and angst and identity and insecurity.

Now, add to THAT, the neurological trauma that our kids have endured, the rewiring that keeps them set on survival and fight-or-flight... and all of the new social skills that are needed and that endless need for attention and affirmation and affection, but the crazy fear that causes them to sabotage it right when they get close. Yeah, add THAT on top. And what you have is "What were we THINKING when we adopted this kid?! I can't do this!"

Now, bring a few more innocent little children into the mix and the level of fear increases quite a bit. I suppose I would feel this way even if the little kids weren't biological. I think I'd fear for any little child. But I'd also be dealing with their damage and hurt and delays.

I mentioned earlier that we asked specifically for children who didn't have any sexual abuse in their background. It ends up that many children come to you with undocumented sexual abuse. This was our case. And not just a little but everything I mentioned in the last chapter on bio families.

Within a few months, our foster child began to manifest interesting behaviors. He was caught in class drawing inappropriate pictures... not of things he necessarily understood, but of things he'd witnessed and other adults could recognize. He used his toys, while playing with our other children, to act out some of these memories. It got scary.

We've always had a distinct set of rules in our home to protect everyone. Doors stay open. Adults stay present. Open conversation. Counseling. But so did our friends. They'd brought in three children while they were beginning their birth family. Their oldest adopted son molested his bio sister. Their second oldest adopted son molested their biological toddler. They had the same rules in place. Followed the same guidelines. And even still.

This breaks my heart.

My sense of security in our plans and rules and vigilance crumbled. We keep them in place and add to our watchfulness... but unless I lock them away, there are no guarantees.

We're not only careful with our own children, but with others' children. We live in a small community and we have an open-door policy. Friends are welcome any time. I often have a few extra around of all ages. And we have to be careful and vigilant. I pray often that this will be one of those horrific cycles in this bio family that ends with our child.

I asked my six- and eight-year-olds about having an adopted brother and sister. Their answers surprised me.

"I like that you can adopt because then you have more brothers and sisters to have fun with. Sometimes, like on your birthdays, and they're gone, they try to get the best thing for you."

—Six-year-old

"The best thing is having more people to play with. I'm happy you adopted because they're fun. I'm sad because sometimes they can be a little annoying."

—Eight-year-old

"My life is better for having an adopted brother and sister because if we didn't adopt I'd only have one brother. And I'd only have him to play with and I wouldn't go to any cafes. Sometimes, they make their rooms cafes and invite us in."

—Six-year-old

I've been afraid that my younger two children have seen my struggle with our older children and taken that on themselves. I don't want my struggle to become theirs. I was so grateful to hear their answers! They have no memory of life without their older brother and sister. This is just life. They have nothing to compare it to in their personal experience. They've been around other sibling sets of all blends and noticed that they also argue and frustrate parents. Sometimes their wisdom and insight at these young ages impresses me.

There was a time when my eight-year-old didn't want to have any children of his own. His reasons were not wanting to change the diapers and how hard it is to raise kids. I don't know if this related directly with his experience watching us try to parent... but I feared it was. I became much more intentional about vocalizing the aspects of parenting that I love. So that in the midst of the difficulties, he hears me saying what I love. I don't know if he'll change his mind but he's got time.

And it's a good practice for me, to think about what I love about being a mother and to say those things out loud. It heals my heart too, like remembering the WHY... pausing to focus on the things I love about this role that tries me to my core.

There have definitely been some scary times in our house. And honestly, if I could go back and do it again, I would wait until our little kids were older. But, as I've heard from other families, if we'd known what was coming, we probably wouldn't have the courage to do it, but what a gift that we stepped in and did it.

So I know without a doubt that if I could go back, I would do it differently. I wouldn't bring older foster/adoptive kids into my home while still having young children. That being said, my little children love their older brother and sister. They don't know a life without them and they wouldn't change it, so why should *I* wish it changed?

Our older kids, in the last year or so, have had new eyes when viewing their little siblings. They see a childhood they should've had but didn't. They see a loving home that evaded them. They came to us at eight and my firstborn is now eight. It's finally comparable. And we can all see how much life happens in eight years. And we missed all of it with them. They missed it too, moving from home to home, missing their families, and growing more confused. Our daughter thought that if she could go from failing in school to straight A's, she'd be able to go home. She achieved her academic goal... but it had never been about that, right?

They see the childhoods of their little siblings and recognize what they've missed. But because they are still too immature to recognize the nuances of how that affects them, they sometimes take it out on the kids. It turns into resentment and anger directed at the little people who aren't to blame.

In fact, none of us are to blame. All the same, they only know they are angry and it has something to do with them. This has led to the older ones smacking the younger ones on the head, making inappropriate comments, telling them and others how "spoiled" their little siblings are and how "neglected" *they* are. Every now and then, they have moments of clarity.

But it reached a point that my littles asked that their older brother and sister don't babysit them. Because they came to this conclusion, and there were some instances of near-danger and harm, we've honored it. Though I have two helpful teenagers at home, we hire a babysitter to watch the little two. After instances of being locked out of the house, of being thrown on the couch with hands around the neck, with moments of verbal abuse… my little kids had enough. They love their big brother and sister, but don't want to be left alone with them.

I don't blame them.

I'm sure my little sister didn't always want to be left alone with me, either.

But most families I know in our age-situation, older kids with younger siblings, have built-in helpers with the kids.

We don't have that.

In fact, it's my oldest who often needs the most supervision.

To be fair, there are birth children who felt it difficult to be older and have foster/adoptive children introduced. My friend was fourteen when her parents adopted two children internationally. For her sixteen-year-old brother, the transition was fine.

For my friend Laura, though, it was extremely difficult. "I was struggling after a rocky experience in junior high. It was the summer prior to my freshmen year in high school. I think that timing is really important. My parents had been waiting a long time and had intended to adopt one younger child, but it seemed to be taking forever so when they saw the photos of Ricky and Stacy they kind of jumped on it. I don't think it was necessarily the kids. I was already heading down a hard road when they came; it just seemed to push me over the edge."

Another friend said, "Our bio kids had a really hard time. Much harder than we were prepared for."

And still another said, "Our firstborn has told us that he was glad to have an older [adopted] brother, even though intellectually the younger child quickly overtook the older."

Regardless of what hindsight has shown us, here we are. We are all in. There's no going back. We pray for each of our kids, are intentional with the unique needs in our home, and keep pouring our everything into this messy family.

Be Vigilant

In our current culture, this should be advice for any parent. In our home, if two or more people are in a room, that door stays open. Kids aren't left home unsupervised. We try to be present wherever in the house kids are hanging out (though I prefer to go hide out in my room!). We are very open with our children and talk through any topics that come up. We try to be proactive in educating them about safety. And, with the knowledge we have about each of them, we try to stay alert for any signs of danger.

Be Intentional

Oftentimes, the children in our homes who don't have challenging behaviors can get lost in the mix. The quiet, the well-behaved, and the easygoing children are often left to themselves while the majority of our energy gets spent on the children requiring so much. I have wept when I've realized how I've short-changed my other kids, depleted from the constant drain of one or two.

It's important my other kids don't miss good, healthy connection with a loving adult (me or my husband) because we're so focused putting out the fires of the ones who already missed it. This takes an intentionality. Sometimes it means I purposefully set aside time for the other children. I don't want them to learn that the loudest, craziest, most draining children get the most attention.

CHAPTER 24

The Challenge of Secondary Trauma

"No one ever told me how sorrow traumatizes your heart, making you think it will never beat exactly the same way again. No one ever told me how grief feels like a wet sock in my mouth. One I'm forced to breathe through, thinking that with each breath I'll come up short and suffocate."

—Sarah Noffke, Awoken

Caring for our children can be difficult, exhausting, draining, and frustrating. I love what Sharon says, "The most difficult part of fostering/adopting is that you are given these children. You care for them, love them, stay up with them when they are running fevers, wipe their tears when they are upset. They are yours in your heart. The uncertainty of where they will end up or even when they will be declared yours is devastating. It is such a beautiful thing to love in this capacity."

And it is. It's beautiful.

And there's a heavy cost.

Some call it "Parenting Burnout." Others know it as "Compassion Fatigue." And still others as "Secondary Traumatic Stress."

Though there are some distinctions between these labels, they share much in common. The common denominator is empathetic people caring for traumatized people. I think parents can experience burnout just being parents. But when we add to parenting a traumatized child and their responses to trauma, we end up traumatized too.

Secondary Trauma Stress (STS) is sometimes confused with burnout. According to Pine, Aronson and Kafry, burnout is "a state of physical, emotional, and mental exhaustion caused by long term involvement in emotionally demanding situations."[1] Unlike STS, burnout can be described as emotional exhaustion, depersonalization, and a reduced feeling of personal accomplishment.

STS, however, is "the emotional duress that results when an individual hears about the firsthand trauma experiences of another. Its symptoms mimic those of post-traumatic stress disorder (PTSD)."[2] STS also includes the emotional duress of a person experiencing trauma because of the manifestations of another person's trauma in their life. "Accordingly, individuals affected by secondary stress may find themselves re-experiencing personal trauma or notice an increase in arousal and avoidance reactions related to the indirect trauma exposure. They may also experience changes in memory and perception; alterations in their sense of self-efficacy; a depletion of personal resources; and disruption in their perceptions of safety, trust, and independence."[2]

Both of these are uncomfortable and frustrating. And I imagine you've found yourself somewhere on the spectrum between severe burnout and secondary trauma. I personally love the language of "compassion fatigue."

We have worn ourselves out caring.

But sometimes it's more than just worn out.

I've been there. Oh, have I been there.

The thing is, I've *never* heard anyone talk about this. And, in fact, when I research it, there is far more information on Secondary Trauma for social workers and therapists and case workers than on the people who live with the kids. This is crazy. I love what Dr. Rachel Remen says in *Kitchen Table Wisdom*, as quoted by Jennifer Middleton: "The expectation that we can be immersed in suffering and loss daily and not be touched by it is as unrealistic as expecting to be able to walk through water without getting wet."[3]

If we are not made to realize that we *will* be affected by the trauma we take under our wing, then we will be much worse for it. We need to be talking about this. It's real and it's affecting many people. People who feel ashamed and embarrassed by what seems like parenting failure when, in reality, it's just "getting wet."

My friend Shelly, a fellow foster and adoptive parent, sums it up well: "The secondary trauma of foster and adoptive parents is real. Some of us have been bit, kicked, slapped, punched, hit, and/or emotionally assaulted because our children can go to such a scary place of fear. We witness it and internalize things as parents. It's so hard to see a child you love so much hurting. It's no fault of their own, but you feel the calling to help heal those wounds you had nothing to do with yourself."

The most vulnerable to STS are those with the additional stresses of caring for traumatized children.

That's us, folks.

A lack of resources and caring support, being empathetic people, and not having enough time to care for ourselves or to recover from the injuries we experience in caring for these kids are leading causes of STS.

As I talked about in Chapter 2, the broken System is not equipped to raise children, let alone provide quality care to the families taking them in. This is especially true of international adoptions, when families come back with a child and there's no system in place to help. They are thrown into parenting after a whirlwind and often embarrassed to ask for help from their community when they've worked so hard to come this far... and then by appearances, not be able to handle it alone.

We are not given the resources we need, any of us, to parent these children alone. If you were or are with a Foster Family Agency, then you definitely have the upper hand. Most FFAs provide *at least* monthly training and a personal social worker who has a small caseload and can be available more frequently. But, even then, after adopting, the support is limited.

And because of our empathy and compassion, one of the reasons we've often chosen to adopt, we take on and carry the burden of our children's trauma as well. As they share their stories, or we hear them from others, or read in the files, as we watch our children struggle through normal tasks because of their emotional blocks and trauma, our hearts break for them. This is not bad! This is what caring people do! But it also means that we take on an additional stress in parenting them, which leads to burnout or STS if we don't have good practices of self-care in place.

Speaking of self-care, it sure is hard to do it when we never have a moment away from the kids, isn't it? I love the idea of self-care. But making it happen in a busy family is very difficult. We feel guilt for leaving our family for a short time to take care of ourselves. For some, it's a nice pedicure, a shopping trip, a nap, a few hours of reading a book, a night out with friends... opportunities to break away from the stress of the norm and laugh a little, escape a little, breathe a lot.

But it's so hard to find and make the time.

This is where Chapter 19 on family, friends, and community is especially important. "When individuals feel valued and are in the presence of others who respect and care for them, they are more capable of tolerating extreme stressors. Clearly this means that the current practices... within a fragmented system with high-turnover—are a set up for increased stress for individuals working in that system."[4] We need the value and presence of our community in order to live under such stress better and longer.

Really, this is the life or death of our family.

It has to come before everything else. Broken, burned out, traumatized parents aren't much good for their traumatized children. In order to be the best that we can be for their needs and dynamics, we have to be healthy.

If we don't make this important, even in the midst of total familial chaos, we can expect mental and physical exhaustion, the unhealthy use of substances to combat stress and to self-comfort, disturbed sleep, feeling numb and distanced from life, feeling less satisfied by work and parenting, irritability and moodiness, physical complaints such as stomachache or headache, intrusive thoughts, chronic fatigue, sadness, anger, poor concentration, second guessing, detachment, emotional exhaustion, fearfulness, shame, and more.

You may have read that list and thought to yourself, *Uhh... I'm already there.*

If that's the case, you need to act immediately. *Go get help.*

It doesn't make you a failure. It doesn't make you a bad parent. It doesn't mean you should never have adopted.

It *does* mean, that like so many others, your brain has also rewired some new pathways in order to deal with the constant high level of stress you've been under. Yes, this happens! Perfectly healthy people, with no unusual emotional or psychiatric history, can find themselves depressed, anxious, emotionally detached from life, moody, or so many other things. It's easy to judge ourselves for this and refuse to let ourselves get help.

I spent a few years feeling exhausted *all the time*. I had physicals done because I was SURE my thyroid was wonky or I had low iron or *something*. But all of my tests came back perfect.

I kept hearing, "You're just a tired mama of four. This is normal."

But my gut kept telling me something wasn't right.

Eventually, I got to where putting one load of laundry in the washer was enough to wipe me out. I'd need to lie down and nap. This was so frustrating! Emotionally, I felt fine. But something physically was debilitating me. I had my youngest home with me half the day. I wanted to be present for her in these last couple of years before school, but I found myself more and more exhausted by the time I retrieved her.

She spent quite a few afternoons sitting beside me in bed reading a book, working on Starfall, an educational website for children, or watching a show. But what I wanted to do was teach her to read, go on bike rides, do crafts together, go on picnics. Every time I heard myself say, "I can't; I'm sooooooo tired," a small piece of me would break inside. I couldn't do what I'd hoped to do.

I went back to my regular doctor. I had a list of things to discuss, one of them being this exhausted. While I was talking, I started crying as I shared how hard it was to parent one of my children. How exhausting. It started as I explained that one of the reasons I'd taken the year off of work was to get enough rest during the day to be rested and present for the challenges my oldest presents when he got home from school. But I seemed to be losing rest during the day, and no good to anyone. My sweet doctor looked into my eyes and said, "YOU are a GOOD mother!"

My youngest sat in the corner wearing a princess dress and rain boots. I was a mess in front of her. All I wanted was to get my laundry done and have a picnic with my girlie. My doctor didn't know if I was a good mother or not, but her words pierced me in a good way.

She gave me a very low dose of an anti-depressant. This seemed a little silly, since I didn't see in myself the symptoms of depression, but I was desperate. "This will give me energy, right?" was all I wanted to know.

"You just need a bridge over this time in your life," she said. *It better be a long bridge*, I thought to myself. *This kid isn't going anywhere.*

I tried it out. About two weeks in, I felt a considerable difference, even for the very low dose I was on. I could function again! I still took periodic naps, but I didn't have the lethargy following me around, dragging me down.

I wished, at that point, that I'd gotten help sooner.

I'd battled the shame. The idea of medication was embarrassing to me. I mean, for other people it's fine. But for me? I'm strong! I'm capable! I'm educated! Did this kid seriously put me on meds?

But once it worked, I realized the truth of it. Yes, the chronic stress for SO MANY YEARS of raising these kids had changed the chemistry in my brain. Stress depletes critical brain chemicals, causing depression.

There are lots of great books and articles on stress, but I found this one to be concise and helpful. In "12 Effects of Chronic Stress on Your Brain," Deane Alban states that "Serotonin-based depression is accompanied by anxiety and irritability, while dopamine-based depression expresses itself as lethargy and lack of enjoyment of life."[5] Both of these are a consequence of chronic stress, which is what we call "parenting our challenging children."

But we're also dealing with loving and losing, Child Protective Services responding to the stories our kids tell people, the judgment of others who don't get it, our own self-judgment, the judgment of the kids themselves, their slander, their anger toward us, their violence toward us, our guilt over the lack of slow attaching, and the reminder that while they are our children... they're also someone else's. Sometimes we see that in their personality, in their predispositions, in their very faces.

We have every right to believe that we have lived under chronic stress for a long, long time. This will manifest differently for each of us, but the end result is much the same... burnout, fatigue, and secondary trauma.

So what do we do? Maybe we don't all need medication,

though I'm now a fan. It gave me the space I needed to "breathe" and recompose. I could handle the challenges without so much emotional tie-in. I could be more objective and feel less hurt by their actions. This gave us all a space to begin working on our healing.

But we *do* all need good support, to create and guard time for ourselves, and a caring community. In "Parenting Children Who Have Experienced Trauma," Laura Phipps wrote, "Taking care of [ourselves] is a must for foster, adoptive, and kin caregivers. If [we] don't, life becomes a spinning top, constantly twirling, and eventually [we] won't have what it takes to help the young people who depend on [us]. Because [we] work with children who have histories of trauma, self-care also means protecting yourself from secondary traumatic stress."[6]

I echo James when he said, "I have been healed so many times over from my own childhood pain because of this gift of being able to love, but the pain of not knowing what will become of them, never seeing their face again, never knowing if they might remember you, never knowing. That is what waked me up some nights in tears, this unanswered love. But what a wonderful pain to have."

It IS a wonderful pain. And there's a cost.

Our very lives.

Our brain chemistry. Our memory. Our energy. Everything.

As Veronica Roth wrote in her novel *Allegiant*, "There are so many ways to be brave in this world. Sometimes, bravery involves laying down your life for something bigger than yourself, or for someone else. Sometimes it involves giving up everything you have ever known, or everyone you have ever loved, for the sake of something greater.

But sometimes it doesn't.

Sometimes it is nothing more than gritting your teeth through pain, and the work of every day, the slow walk toward a better life.

That is the sort of bravery I must have now."

Take Care of Yourself

The best thing we can do for our child and for our family is to take care of ourselves. There are many great resources on self-care. As a counselor, it's one of the first things I recommend to people in high-stress situations. Connect with a life-giving activity and *make the time for it.* I know this can sound impossible. But you have to do it. Get a babysitter. Take time off work. Whatever. For me, this might be a weekend retreat with some girlfriends with a hot tub, good food, and lots of laughter.

For you, maybe it's time in the garden, art studio, or running each morning. It's also about knowing your limits. I've realized with some children I've parented, that I can only do so many straight days with them before I'm on borderline losing it. This isn't good for them or for me. So now I know that I need a plan for any school break that is that many days or longer. Maybe they need to work. Or spend time with a family member. Something to take care of each of us. You can do this. You must do this.

1. A. Pine, E. Aronson, and D. Kafry, Burnout: From Tedium to Personal Growth (New York, NY: Free Press, 1981).

2. The National Child Traumatic Stress Network, "Secondary Traumatic Stress: A Fact Sheet for Child-Serving Professionals" (2011), 1-2, accessed October `0, 2015, www.nctsn.org/sites/default/files/assets/pdfs/secondary_traumatic_tress.pdf

3. Jennifer Middleton, "Addressing Secondary Trauma and Compassion Fatigue in Work with Older Veterans: An Ethical Imperative, Journal of Geriatric Care Management (Spring 2015), accessed October 10, 2015, www.gcmjournal.org/2015/05/15/addressing-secondary-trauma-and-compassion-fatigue-in-work-with-older-veterans-an-ethical-imperative/

4. Bruce D. Perry, The Cost of Caring: Secondary Traumatic Stress and the Impact of Working with High-Risk Children and Families (Houston, TX: ChildTrauma Academy, 2003), 8, accessed October 10, 2015, www.community.nsw.gov.au/docswr/_assets/main/lib100056/reading_perry.pdf

5. Deane Alban, "12 Effects of Chronic Stress on Your Brain," Be Brain Fit (blog), accessed October 10, 2015, www.bebrainfit.com/effects-chronic-stress-brain/

6. Laura Phipps, "Parenting Children Who Have Experienced Trauma," Fostering Perspectives 18, no. 1 (November 2013), accessed October 10, 2015, www.fosteringperspectives.org/fpv18n1/Phipps.htm

CHAPTER 25

❧

Conclusion

❧

"Because God is never cruel, there is a reason for all things. We must know the pain of loss; because if we never knew it, we would have no compassion for others, and we would become monsters of self-regard, creatures of unalloyed selfinterest. The terrible pain of loss teaches humility to our prideful kind, has the power to soften uncaring hearts, to make a better person of a good one."

— Dean Koontz, The Darkest Evening of the Year

All behavior is based on a deep-seated belief or purpose. The great "Why?" in our life guides our decisions and our actions. As a behavior analyst, I saw this all the time in my work with families and children. One kid would throw up to avoid doing a chore. It worked. His mom was naturally distracted with his vomit and let him off the hook. He believed, deep down, that in order to survive in life, he needed to manipulate and coerce.

It starts young. There's a big "WHY?" behind the person you decide to marry (or the one you refuse), behind the job you take, the house you buy, the education you pursue. It's behind the reasons you feel lonely or anxious. Our underlying beliefs are responsible for *a lot*.

Often, returning our eyes to the reasons we set out on a certain adventure can rekindle our excitement for said adventure. My husband and I were in a rough patch one year when our anniversary came. Neither of us were very excited to celebrate it. Some friends invited us for dinner. Naturally, they asked, "So, how'd you guys meet?" They didn't know that we were struggling. We were putting up a decent front. You know, plastered smiles and conversation, though we hadn't had any for each other for a while.

My husband began to share our love story. And I intermittently corrected him. And together, we wove an image for our friends of our journey, birthed out of mutual friendship, community, love for the world and culture and language, and ultimately each other.

As we finished our story, my husband leaned over and whispered, "It's so nice remembering how we came together, isn't it?" and he grabbed my hand. This was the most positive contact we'd had in a couple of weeks. And he was right. Somehow, remembering all of the reasons we'd chosen each other made the current conflict seem small.

We need these moments in our experience with foster care and adoption, too. I have pounded my head into my bed and wracked my brain for the WHY! Why did we decide to do this? Why did we invite all of this pain? The judgment from others? The fear? The anxiety? Our lives had been peachy until we took these kids in... So why did we do it?

It's often a muddy, murky blur. Oftentimes, I have to step out of the cloud to see our original vision again. A friend needs to ask me, "Why did you adopt?" to get me tell that love story.

Or I have to lean over to my husband and ask, "Remind me; what were we thinking again? Were we crazy?" I'm going to bet, if you're reading this book, that you've been there too. You've reached such depths of hurt, confusion, betrayal, embarrassment, and anger that you can't remember whatever inspired you to invite this heart-wrenching ache into your home. Their sweet little faces morph into monsters and we only see the trouble they cause... forgetting why we started down this road to begin with.

We have to know our WHY. If we lose it... we lose ourselves. We lose our kids. We do more damage to everyone while we flounder in the sea of all-things-disturbing. Ever met the foster or adoptive parents whose home seems in constant turmoil? And yet they keep taking in one more kid? They smile? They say they love it? They don't seem nearly as messy as you? That's a parent with the WHY tattooed to their inner eyelids.

Yes, it's hard. Yes, it hurts. Yes, they've been bitten, peed on, cursed at... but it was never about that. It was always about their WHY.

So what's your WHY? What's your love story with these kids? What was the original spark that set you on fire for adoption (ha, and sometimes literally!)? Maybe you watched the news or had a friend who worked in Social Services and you heard that statistic that in 2013 there were 402,378 children in foster care in America and far fewer certified foster homes to take them.

Or maybe you'd never considered foster care or adoption until your family member or friend asked you to take in their child. Or maybe you just love kids so much you couldn't imagine having enough of them... and your big heart opened your home to any orphan needing a family.

Maybe you experienced infertility and, wanting desperately to be a parent, you reached out to mother or father the child of a stranger. Or maybe you yourself were fostered or adopted and you want to return the love... help another kid the way you had been helped. Perhaps you felt a spiritual calling and responsibility to care for other humans regardless of the cost.

There are so many possible reasons that your heart ached and your fingers signed the dotted line, and your life changed forever. Go back to yours. Sit and think about it. Why did you do this? Don't think about what you didn't know at the time... just the reason you opened your doors and your heart. This will change everything.

Our WHY is probably as much a combination of things as yours. Mine began as I pursued my degree in social work and had internships at Child Protective Services and Health and Human Services. I read about the need. I saw the need first hand.

I met the kids and their families, both biological families and foster families. I worked in a group home for males and a group home for teen moms. I worked as a facilitator and case manager for wrap-around programs, community based programs, and children needing therapeutic services. I worked in counseling centers and foster agencies. I worked as a behavior analyst for families with children who had emotional and developmental delays.

I had seen it all.

Or so I thought.

I often thought to myself, *There is such a great need... if I could just provide one more good home, even just one, then I'm part of the solution.*

My husband worked in a low-performing school in a part of town that had terribly high rates of single-parent families and foster children. He was their teacher. Day in and day out, he often spent more time with these kids than their own parents (foster or otherwise). He saw their educational needs, their deficits, their strengths. He often thought to himself, *If I can provide one good home for these kids... I can be an advocate for their learning and coach them through school. I can be part of the solution.*

What if we could help? We had the education. We had the experience. We were informed. We didn't have any other children yet... but we were good at what we did.

The foundation of it all, though, was our belief in God as an adoptive Father. We were guided in purpose by our faith. There's a verse in the Bible that says, "Religion that God our Father accepts as pure and faultless is this: to look after orphans and widows in their distress and to keep oneself from being polluted by the world" (James 1:27).

We understand this verse to mean that we have a duty before God to care for orphans, even social orphans, in their distress. Being removed from your home is definitely distressing. Being raised by the government is distressing. Being passed around? Distressing. We felt it was our duty and calling and privilege to care for these kiddos. This is why we became foster parents: We were informed, experienced, educated, able, and we heard in God's Word that we were to take care of these kids.

WHY adopt them? Wouldn't fostering have been enough? Why this extra step of making these strangers' kids ours FOREVER? Some of you started here, skipping right over foster care. It's a huge commitment, and while we don't do it lightly, we often have NO idea what is really in store for us. But there is much about foster care that inspires adoption. Government involvement is ridiculous.

And we just couldn't see taking in a kid who was never going back to their parents and saying, "Sorry kid, we'll only be your parents for a little while." I could only imagine how devastating that must feel... how worthless kids must feel when people pass them on. We didn't want to perpetuate that in any child's life. We wanted to keep a kid for as long as possible, and we never wanted to be the reason that they had to go.

Again, our faith teaches us that God bestows on us His unconditional love… that no matter where we've been or what we do, He will love us forever. And not just love us, but like us. We wanted to offer that same kind of gift to any kid who came to our home and say to them, "No matter what you've done or where you've been or who your family is… we will not give up on you."

Because this was done for us. "For those who are led by the Spirit of God are the children of God. The Spirit you received does not make you slaves, so that you live in fear again; rather, the Spirit you received brought about your adoption to sonship. And by Him we cry, 'Abba, Father'" (Romans 8:14-15).

I'm adopted! Not in the human sense, but spiritually. And I did nothing to deserve it. I can't earn it. I can't be worthy of it. I was destined for horror, and Someone pulled me out. Gave me a chance at a different outcome, no strings attached. The least I can do, out of my deep gratitude, is let that love and unconditional acceptance overflow into the lives of those around me.

On the dark, hard, hopeless days, I have to go back to our WHY. I have to remember that there is something bigger, something deep and meaningful, behind why we chose this wild ride. On the days when I wish we hadn't, I beg God or my husband to remind me why we did this. I'm recentered when I remember that it was to reflect God's love to these kids. A love I don't deserve but live in freely. I'm reinspired when I remember that we didn't adopt for our comfort, but to be a chance at hope and change and a future for even one. I can walk through one more day, one more minute, when I remember that this was because the alternatives for these kids were much worse… and even when I think I really, really don't like them… I do.

I love them too much to leave them to the alternatives.

ABOUT THE AUTHOR

Marcy M. Pusey, CRC, is a graduate of Fresno Pacific University. She completed her postgraduate counseling education at California State University, Fresno with training in the application of counseling skills to assist individuals with physical, mental, developmental, cognitive, and emotional disabilities to achieve the best quality of life possible.

She is currently a clinical counselor for a missionary community in southern Germany. Marcy's counseling work over the last sixteen years has included children, adolescents, adults, families, and couples. She has provided care through private practices, group homes, foster family agencies, community based services, and wrap-around programs.

She is a passionate, deep-thinking writer, wife, and mommy living the serendipitous moments of God's divine intentions. Her writing has appeared in newspapers, magazines, children's books, and books for adults. She lives in the Black Forest of Germany with her husband and children (two of whom are adopted through foster care). Marcy blogs inspirationally about her work, writing, and other resources at **www.marcypusey.com.**

URGENT PLEA!

Thank you for purchasing my book

**I really appreciate all of your feedback,
and love hearing what you have to say.**

**I need your input to make
the next version better.**

**Please leave me
a helpful REVIEW on Amazon**

Thanks so much!!

Proof

Made in the USA
Columbia, SC
07 August 2017